BUCKINGHAM PALACE

I am pleased to be Patron of the 1992 USAAF Reunion which will commemorate and reinforce fifty years of remarkable friendship between two nations. During my visits to the United States I have been thrilled and encouraged by the welcome and the great kindness that has been shown to me by the American people. I have become very conscious that there is a special relationship between the British and the Americans. The presence of more than half a million American servicemen here in the 1940s helped to strengthen that relationship.

I hope that many veterans of the United States Army Forces will return to England in 1992 together with their families. A warm welcome awaits them and I hope that I may have the opportunity of meeting some of them myself.

Andrew

THE AMERICANS RETURN TO STANSTED

Fifty years on, the Americans are returning to London Stansted. On June 16 1992 American Airlines will launch a daily scheduled service from Chicago.

The opening of a new $700 million development has transformed Stansted into one of Europe's most modern airports with an award-winning terminal that is light, airy and easy to use with all passenger facilities on one level.

The 41 minute Stansted Express rail link into the heart of the City of London makes the airport a popular choice with both business and leisure passengers. Stansted also features car rental desks with Hertz, Avis, Budget and Europcar.

What better way to start your reunion visit than to land at one of the original USAAF airfields?

For further details please call...
American Airlines on 800 624 6262.
or London Stansted Airport on 010 44 279 662714

50TH ANNIVERSARY
LONDON
STANSTED
AIRPORT
1942 – 1992

ontents

Editors:
Melanie J Faux
Jane Sullivan

Advertising:
Madison Bell Ltd,
London

*Front cover shows
Captain Cunningham
and crew of the
305th BG standing
beside the B-17 Flying
Fortress 'Patches',
5 June 1943.*

Designed by
Melanie J Faux

Reproduction by
Thetford Photo Litho

Printed in England
by Spottiswoode
Ballantyne Printers
Ltd

Published by the
East Anglia Tourist
Board, Toppesfield
Hall, Hadleigh,
Suffolk IP7 5DN

Every effort has
been made to ensure
accuracy in this
publication. The
East Anglia Tourist
Board cannot accept
responsibility for
any error or
omission which
may have occurred.

© The East Anglia
Tourist Board

With grateful thanks to:
*Dave Brett, The BT Museum, Claire Burge, Coca-Cola Great Britain, R J Collis,
Colours Partnership, Lalli Coppinger, CPC (United Kingdom) Ltd, Phyllis duBois, Pat Everson,
George H Fox, Roger A Freeman, Terry Gladwell, Guinness Brewing GB, John Hamlin,
The Image Factory, Ian McLachlan, John Mills, Dave Osborne, Caroline Putus, Rebel Air Museum,
Connie Richards, Smart Graphics, The Taxi Museum,
Terence Dalton Ltd (for excerpts from The Friendly Invasion, pages 18-21, 32-35, 58, 60-61, 63-64, 68- 69),
Hugh Walker, Herbert Watson, Norman Wells.*

Just what are we celebrating in 1992? And why? Natural questions for the uninitiated. In simple terms we are commemorating the coming together of the peoples of two nations occasioned by the arrival of the United States forces in 1942. The 1992 celebrations are not an excuse for flag-waving over a past victory, or to indulge in re-fighting the Second World War in the air. Rather, the event is to mark the impact of more than a half million young American servicemen and women upon the East Anglian scene; the friendly invasion.

By the time of D-Day, June 1944, more than half of the USAAF's combat strength was concentrated in this island, most in the greater East Anglian area. Associations with the local people produced many lasting friendships - and some sixty thousand marriages. During near three years of air operations from England, more than fifty thousand airmen were missing or killed in action and many still have their last resting place in British soil. Airmen cannot return to battlefields in the sky to pay respects to comrades who fell and so the focal point of interest has been the old wartime bases and villages nearby. It is in these villages that a special bond developed between those who served and those whose 'neighbourhood' had been invaded.

Now, a half century on from that first coming, the occasion arises to mark a notable wartime relationship.

Roger A Freeman (Historian and Author)

This is about an invasion - not hostile, but friendly. It began just 50 years ago, at a time when one small nation stood with her back to the wall and needed help against her enemies. Not for the first time, servicemen and women from the United States came over to Britain to lend a hand. Their enthusiasm and weight of numbers went a very long way towards ending the Second World War.

For the people of Britain, 1940 was the darkest hour of the war. Throughout the Blitz they had faced up to Germany, becoming increasingly isolated as Europe was being overrun. Although the army had been rescued from Dunkirk, much of its arms and equipment had perforce been abandoned. By 1941 the people were hungry, tired and battered, and apart from help given by the Commonwealth countries, they stood alone.

And yet, not entirely alone. Despite its official stance of neutrality, the United States was already giving practical assistance in a variety of ways. In December 1940 Congress agreed to supply on Lend-Lease the arms and vehicles Britain so urgently needed. Also, while most US citizens didn't want to become involved in another European conflict, several hundred risked losing their citizenship by volunteering to serve with British forces. Many flew with the Royal Air Force's special 'Eagle Squadrons' in Fighter Command, while non-uniformed engineers and medics came over and helped on several British bases - purely on 'the buddy principle'.

The events of 7th December 1941 changed all that; Japan attacked the US naval base at Pearl Harbor in Hawaii, war was declared on Japan and four days later Germany and Italy backed up their Far East ally by declaring war on the United States. For the United States Pearl Harbor marked the beginning of hostilities on two fronts; for Britain it was like the arrival of the US Cavalry with much needed relief. On 8th December President Roosevelt cabled Winston Churchill: "Today all of us are in the same boat with you ... and it is a ship which will not and can not be sunk". After this, Churchill admitted he "went to bed and slept the sleep of the saved and thankful".

By the spring of 1942 US troop landings in Britain were well under way and all summer passenger liners including 'Queen Elizabeth' and 'Queen Mary' zig-zagged across the Atlantic, dodging U-boats and carrying up to 18,000 soldiers and airmen at a time. While many of the military went on to North Africa, about 30,000 USAAF spent their first winter on British bases, mostly in a flat farming area near to Europe - East Anglia.

It was the USAAF that had the most permanent association with the UK during the Second World War and whose members generally made the most impression on the British populace. Some of them not only served here for three full years, but at the same location. By June 1943 the number of US airmen in Britain was over 100,000 and by D-Day peaked at 436,000. The largest concentration was in the greater East Anglian area where most of the 8th Air Force and some of the 9th were located on near a hundred bases.

The task of building enough airfields, warehouses, repair depots and accommodation for these forces was monumental. Britain already had 50 million people crammed into an area the size of New Mexico and half Texas - and needed to grow all her food as well! At its peak, the combined American presence was equal to the population of Maryland. The US and British governments worked flat-out together to provide the necessary facilities, but the local people and the visitors had to learn to live together. At that time few people in either country had any real idea about the other, apart

from myths absorbed at the cinema. Americans tended to think of the British as mi'lords, butlers, Scotland Yard types or London low-life in thick fog. This was almost as off-beam as British notions of covered wagons, stetsons, Chicago striped suits and Hollywood mansions for everyone in America. Expectations on both sides were often confounded by reality. Incoming Americans were handed their government's 'Short Guide to Great Britain' which warned them about pecularities and sensitive aspects of life over here. 'Meet the Americans' was the British attempt to explain the American psyche and values to the people who would be in contact with them. However, these worthy attempts at public relations could not foresee the many ways in which both sides would rub up against each other and resolve their differences in outlook, conduct and standard of living.

There exists an enormous archive of anecdotes and snapshots about our friendly invasion, collected from both US and British sources, and it is on this that much of this souvenir guide has been based. There are funny stories, where we laugh at ourselves and each other, human stories showing the innate kindliness of ordinary folk, happy stories of personal achievement and life enjoyed even in wartime, sad stories of buddies who didn't make it home and romantic stories which have resulted in thousands of permanent Anglo-American family links.

For those who missed out on this particular time, these stories and others, which are still emerging from our veterans' memories, will serve to bring alive and into focus what it is all about and why it still matters. This book is our tribute to those days, to the men and women who lived through them and to the abiding friendships forged at that time.

1992 is the anniversary of the first USAAF arrivals in East Anglia, and we want the occasion to be a memorable one. There is a full programme of events, from the two-day Reunion Airshow at Duxford to exhibitions, receptions and parties, to village get-togethers of friends who have kept in touch for half a century. We hope you will see a lot, have a laugh, perhaps shed a tear, and enjoy it all. ■

RETURN TO
ENGLAND
1942-1992

As the title implies, the United States Army Air Forces was part of the United States Army. However, it was semi-autonomous and the main American air arm of the Second World War. Following the USA becoming involved in hostilities in December 1941, plans for combat deployment brought the major concentration of its air forces to the UK, both to support a proposed cross-Channel invasion of emeny occupied Europe and to conduct a bombing campaign against his war industry. The headquarters for the UK based air units was designated the 8th Air Force, but soon after its establishment it was given the task of forming and equipping a new air force, the 12th, which was to support the Allied landings in North West Africa. The 12th Air Force departed late in 1942 taking most of the 8th Air Force units with it. Thereafter the principle mission of the 8th was strategic attack of enemy war industry using B-17 Fortress and B-24 Liberator bombers.

In the autumn of 1943 the 8th's tactical command, with air units chiefly dedicated to the support of ground forces, was designated the 9th Air Force. The 9th Air Force was rapidly expanded and in both personnel and aircraft nearly equalled the 8th in total strength. At the time of the cross-Channel invasion in June 1944, half the total combat strength of the USAAF was with the 8th and 9th Air Forces in England.

8th Air Force

In terms of men and machines, the 8th Air Force of the Second World War was the largest air striking force ever committed to battle. It could despatch 3,000 bombers and fighters on a single day's operations, which meant that more than 20,000 young men would take to the sky and go out to battle from East Anglia. The despatch of these operations presented a never to be forgotten spectacle for people who lived in the region, although at the time it became almost commonplace. Apart from the dramatic sights in the sky, the noise from thousands of unsilenced aero engines flooded the countryside: rare were the occasions when the throb and drone were absent.

The first seven officers of the 8th Air Force arrived in the United Kingdom two months after the United States was brought into the war. Other personnel followed in an ever mounting stream, the first complete units sailing the Atlantic at the end of April 1942 and disembarking on 11th May. Air operations began in June when American airmen flew for experience with the RAF and the first participation in strength took place on Independence Day when six crews joined the RAF in a light bomber attack on airfields in the Netherlands. Heavy bomber operations commenced in August that year and began the principal commitment. However, diversion delayed the planned force and it was not until June 1944 that the 8th reached its maximum strength.

At that time it had 41 heavy bomber airfields, 15 fighter and 2 reconnaisance, plus several providing support roles. Divided into three divisions, and amounting to air forces within an air force, the 1st Division occupied airfields mostly near Huntingdon and was equipped with B-17 Fortresses, the 2nd Division was in central and south Norfolk flying B-24 Liberators and the 3rd Division, with a mixture of Fortresses and Liberators used mainly Suffolk bases. The fighter units originally flew P-47 Thunderbolt and P-38 Lightning aircraft, but it converted to the superior P-51 Mustang by the end of hostilities.

In addition to the airfield bases, the 8th Air Force controlled a variety of support installations such as maintenance depots, ordnance dumps and transport facilities. Nearly a quarter of a million men and women were serving with the 8th at peak inventory and during the course of its units' stay in the United Kingdom - which extended to nearly four years in some cases - it is estimated a total of 350,000 personnel came under its direction.

The scale and intensity of the 8th Air Force's war is indicated by the fact that half the awards of America's highest decoration for bravery, the Medal of Honor, made to members of the USAAF went to airmen serving with or for the 8th. Nearly half the casualties sustained by the USAAF were from the 8th and there are many other facts that help make this air force one of the most famous ever. ■

Further information on the 8th and 9th Air Forces can be obtained by contacting the addresses shown on page 77.

8th Air Force

9th Air Force

9th Air Force

At the outset, three priorities for the 9th Air Force were determined: to gain and hold air superiority; to disrupt lines of communication; and to destroy enemy forces at the front line in close cooperation with the troops on the ground.

The 9th Air Force was re-formed in England in October 1943 after a period of service in the Middle East. Initially its main operational four units were medium bombardment groups taken over from the 8th Air Force. Over the next few months seven more bomber groups arrived from the United States and there were then three flying A-20 Bostons and eight flying B-26 Marauders, all based on Essex airfields. The task of the bombardment groups was, at first, to 'soften up' the enemy defences and communications in France in advance of the forthcoming invasion of Europe, an event most people knew would happen but few knew where or when. Soon after the invasion a few of the bombardment groups moved from Essex to airfields near the south coast of England.

The work of the bombardment groups was supplemented by the efforts of three Tactical Air Commands, whose fighter groups used P-38 Lightnings, P-47 Thunderbolts and P-51 Mustangs. These aircraft were mostly based on airfields in the south of England, many of them on specially constructed Advanced Landing Grounds in Kent in order to lengthen dwell times over France before and during the invasion. Construction of these landing grounds provided valuable experience for the troops of the engineer aviation battalions, many of whom were among the first members of the 9th Air Force to land in Normandy on D-Day.

As soon as the engineers had completed usable strips close to the Normandy beachhead, fighter groups began to operate from them, greatly increasing the number of sorties carried out. Soon the bombardment groups also began to leave England to take up positions on French airstrips and also increased their effect.

Supporting the bombers and fighters were a small number of Tactical Reconnaissance Groups, whose main task was to provide up-to-the-minute intelligence on the enemy forces' disposition. For this vital work, reconnaissance versions of the P-51 and the P-38 were used. Indirectly also giving support were two squadrons of P-61 Black Widow night fighters, which flew night interdiction missions.

Apart from its strike aircraft, the 9th Air Force was the operator of the most formidable troop-carrying force ever assembled. On D-Day, no less than 56 squadrons in fourteen troop carrier groups were in action carrying para troops or towing gliders. Almost all the aircraft were C-47 Skytrains, and the gliders mainly Waco CG-4s, plus a number of British-built Horsas. This force, based on airfields in Lincolnshire, Nottinghamshire, Wiltshire, Somerset and Devon, later took part in the airborne operations to Arnhem. A few C-46 Commandos were added to the Force before the end of the war.

As in any military formation, the work put in by the personnel behind the scenes, usually unrecorded, was invaluable. To deal with the massive task of provisioning, servicing, assembly and generally making sure that the 9th Air Force functioned properly, IX Air Force Service Command was formed. Among its many tasks were the assembly of aircraft such as P-51s and P-38s shipped over the Atlantic into British ports and the assembly of over 4000 CG-4 gliders, each of which arrived in five large packing cases. The record for glider assembly was 100 in a single day. IX Air Force Service Command also set up a series of Tactical Air Depots, where aircraft of specific types were given major overhauls.

During the 25 months of its existence, the 9th grew from a tiny nucleus to over 200,000 personnel in 45 combat groups and a vast selection of non-combat units, flying over 1,100 bomber aircraft, a huge number of fighters and 3,000 troop-carrying aircraft. The men and women who served in the 9th Air Force can rightly be proud of their efforts and attainments. ■

A group of happy fighter pilots crowded on a P-47 Thunderbolt.

Airfields of the 40s

Old Buckenham, 1992.

A few years ago I had a chance to visit Old Buckenham again. A train ride and a taxi ride landed me at our old base. The base was gone. The memories remained. I stood where the runways used to be and I cried a little because I could see so clearly so many close friends who didn't get to go home again. If I should get another chance to return to Old Buck I will gladly do so, though I know full well that I will cry again and I will see my crew again and I will see our plane again.

John Best, Massachusetts

Key to Location

O = 8th Air Force

● = 9th Air Force

◑ = Both

Warton

Burtonwoo

High Ercall

Atcham O

Colerne ●
● Charmy Do

Keevil ◑

● Weston Zoyland

● Merryfield

Dunkeswell
○   ● Upottery

● Exeter

Holm

● Warmwell
WEYMOUTH

Goxhill

Kirton in Lindsey

LINCOLN

Balderton ● ● Fulbeck

● Barkston Heath
Bottesford
Langar ● ● Folkingham

● Saltby

● North Witham

● Cottesmore

HUNSTANTON

KING'S LYNN

Attlebridge

Horsham St. Faith

Spanhoe ● ○ King's Cliffe
Deenethorpe ○ PETERBOROUGH
Grafton Underwood ○ ● Polebrook
Harrington ● Glatton

Wendling

Shipdham
North Pickenham
Bodney ○ Hethel
Watton
Deopham Green
East Wretham ○ Snetterton Heath

Molesworth ○ Alconbury
Podington ○ Chelveston
● Kimbolton
● Little Staughton
NORTHAMPTON
Thurleigh

ELY

Old Buckenham
Knettishall
Honington

Great Ashfield

BEDFORD
CAMBRIDGE ○ Bottisham

Bury St. Edmunds

Rattlesden

NORWICH
GREAT
YARMOUTH

Seething

Hardwick
Tibenham
Thorpe Abbotts

Eye

Metfield

Halesworth

Horham

Mendlesham

Framlingham

Leiston

Debach

Fowlmere ○ Duxford
Bassingbourn
Steeple Morden

Little Walden

Ridgewell

Lavenham

Wattisham

Martlesham Heath

Nuthampstead ○ Debden
Wethersfield
Stansted ● Gosfield
Great Dunmow ● Earls Colne
Andrew's Field
Matching Green
Chipping Ongar
Boreham ● Rivenhall

Sudbury
IPSWICH
Raydon
Wormingford
Boxted

Birch
COLCHESTER
CHELMSFORD

FELIXSTOWE
HARWICH

Cheddington

OXFORD
Mount Farm ○ ○ Chalgrove
● Grove
Membury
● Welford
Ramsbury

Bovingdon

SOUTHEND-ON-SEA

Aldermaston
Greenham Common

Heston
LONDON

Thruxton
● Andover
● Chilbolton
Middle Wallop

MAIDSTONE

Headcorn
Staplehurst
Lashenden ● Ashford
High Halden ● Kingsnorth
Woodchurch

DOVER

SOUTHAMPTON

Stoney Cross

Bisterne Beaulieu
Lymington
Winkton
Christchurch

Westhampnett

PORTSMOUTH

Merston

BRIGHTON

ROYAL
TUNBRIDGE
WELLS

HASTINGS

o support the Anniversary Reunion.

AT&T has helped people around the world keep in touch for over a century.

Available from over 100 countries world-wide, *AT&T* **USADirect** *Service* is the only service that puts you in touch with an AT&T operator in the States.

Use *AT&T* **USADirect** *Service* to call home and begin to enjoy the convenience of a century's experience.

AT&T makes it easy for you to call home from England.

AT&T **USADirect**® *Service.*

When calling back to the States from England, just dial **0800-89-0011**.* You can use your *AT&T Calling Card*, or call collect. By using the *AT&T Calling Card*, you'll be able to dial directly to the States with new AT&T automated card calling. And *AT&T* **USADirect**® *Service* is available from over 100 countries worldwide. It's just another way AT&T is there to help you from practically anywhere in the world. If you would like more information on *AT&T* **USADirect**® *Service*, call us at **071-355-6079**.

*Public phones require coin or card

AT&T
The right choice.

AT&T **USADirect**® *Service from the UK*
Dial 0800 - 89 - 0011

Nineteen forty two was the year that thousands of young American servicemen suddenly 'dropped in' on Great Britain to stay a while. If they had come from the planet Mars they couldn't have seemed more alien to the unsuspecting British natives. Even the possibility of a German invasion hadn't stirred up as much excitement as did the arrival of the high spirited Yanks!

A Nostalgic Look Back

In East Anglia sedate little villages and quiet market towns near newly constructed airbases, where tradition had remained undisturbed for generations, were overnight transformed into lively bustling communities, streets crowded and echoing with the unfamiliar sounds of American accents from every state in the USA. The United States Army Air Forces had arrived!

At first they had very little free time, but as they were granted passes to leave the airbases they appeared everywhere in the towns and villages, eager to get acquainted with their new

One had to admit, they had a certain kind of charm!

surroundings. They strolled in groups, taking in the sights and commenting on everything they saw, for all the world like happy tourists, engaging in conversation anyone who even looked at them, which was just about everyone for they were the centre of attraction. Their unusually forward manner startled the more traditionally formal Britishers whose social practices didn't include waylaying perfect strangers in the street to chat with them. Well, those friendly Yanks did, and there were many Brits who enjoyed it. It was refreshing they said. And one had to admit, they had a certain kind of charm!

Some other folks didn't agree, and failed to appreciate the Americans' robust idea of fun. Comments such as "they're undisciplined" "girl chasers" ... "a noisy lot" were voiced here and there. This was true of some but not all of them. There were those who approached this 'foreign' land a little more cautiously, preferring to feel their way as onlookers before being participants in the passing show. All were lonesome for the sight of someone or something familiar to remind them of home. Americans all, they were the personification of America's diversified 'melting pot' and the war was giving us a chance to know them in a way we never could have done otherwise.

Maybe, in our ignorance, we in Britain had expected Americans to be more like ourselves. After all, didn't we speak the same language -

more or less - and didn't they used to be British? A little World War II British guidebook on 'Meeting the Americans' reminded us that they had also once fought a war to get away from us and although they might not be thought of exactly as foreigners, the little book explained that they certainly weren't another kind of Englishman either!

Getting to know the Americans was a memorable highlight of the war. They provided excitement and brought fun back into our lives at the time we most needed it, when we were suffering greatly from the deprivations of three years of war. They livened up our dreary towns and introduced a new world to us.

We learned to understand each other's cultural differences, but were also surprised to find out how much alike we were in many ways. When we opened up our homes and hospitality to them they responded wholeheartedly and gradually became a very large part of our lives. Many were in England for as long as three years, plenty of time to form a special bonding and lasting friendships.

Lucky Strike cigarette packet circa 1942-1945. Illustration by Colours Partnership.

"The rest-pause that refreshes"

DRINK Coca-Cola

The GIs had a great liking for children who needed no encouragement to make their acquaintance. Their faces would light up when their American friends dug down into their pockets and brought out never ending supplies of candy and chewing gum. No one will ever forget the catch phrase "any gum chum?"

Many East Anglians who befriended the air crews became familiar with their aircraft, and learned to identify them by the slogans and drawings of exotic females that decorated them, some of which were suggested by Varga girl posters popular in the US around that era. These drawings and paintings, though overly exotic, were cleverly artistic and were usually accompanied by such descriptive titles as 'Virgin on the Verge', 'Fancy Nancy', 'Piccadilly Lily' and 'Anytime Annie'. Some were depicted in their underwear, and some nude, but at all times they were beautiful, never vulgar. The young air crews demanded the finest. It was fantasy, and they deserved to dream a little as a release from the stress of days and weeks of continual bombing missions. Their happy-go-lucky attitude belied their staunch dedication to duty, which proved itself continuously during the weeks and months of dangerous bombing missions. They didn't exhibit their stiff upper lip like our British men,

No one will ever forget the catchphrase "any gum chum?"

but it was there, hidden, and showed itself when needed, which was just about every day. The support groups, the ground crews (the unsung heroes) were always there, watching, waiting and working to keep them flying. They all worked hard and played hard. They acted nonchalant. That was the American way and we learned to love and understand the way they were.

We owe much to those brave young men who flew the planes and turned the winds of war in our favour. When the war was won and it came time for the Americans to leave our shores many people whose lives they had touched were saddened to see them go. It was rather like parting with members of ones family and, in a sense, they had been a big part of Britain's family for three or more years.

But the Yanks of World War II never forgot their sojourn in the UK and have returned in great numbers through the years, many with their British wives. I am one of them. ■

Lalli Coppinger

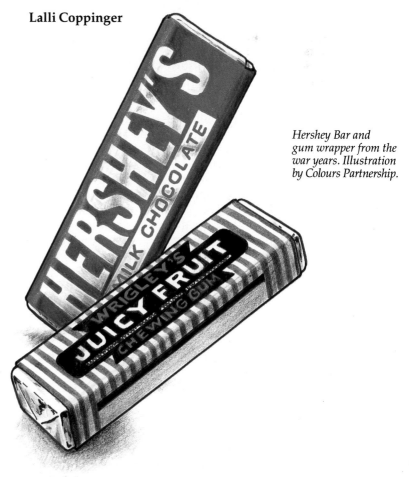

Hershey Bar and gum wrapper from the war years. Illustration by Colours Partnership.

American coffee was strong by British tastes, their own brew being considered no better than 'muddy water' by the GIs. The coming of the Yanks gave people in the UK their introductions to chilli-con-carne, peanut butter, Coke and other delights of the American palate. As far as can be gauged few natives became enthusiastic about their allies' tastes.

orities and when with British friends most Americans were considerate enough to only take frugal helpings. Gifts of foodstuffs were another feature of such visits. In any case, much British food was not to American tastes. Those who had experienced meals in British messes considered them atrocious or, at best, unappetizing - as did many British servicemen. War-

Fifty years on this meal board informs visitors to Horham airfield of the regular meal hours.

Contact and friendships quickly highlighted differences in tastes, customs and habits. Food and drink was a noticeable area; the British quickly learning that coffee and doughnuts, more correctly dough rings, were as big an obsession with the newcomers as tea was with them.

Eating with the fork in the right hand, yet transferring it to the left every time the knife was taken up, was an American habit which intrigued their hosts; it was so out of keeping with the common sense behaviour that characterised US practice. Indeed more than one USAAF flyer, who had been shot down over enemy occupied territory and escaped capture, finally gave himself away by eating with a fork in the right hand. As for the content of the plate,

The coming of the Yanks gave people in the UK their introductions to chilli-con-carne, peanut butter, Coke and other delights of the American palate.

the uninitiated Briton was surprised to see GIs add jam or tinned fruit to meat and vegetables; mixtures of sweet and savoury being a common choice. The strictures of food rationing in the UK were impressed on GIs by the USAAF auth-

time food in the UK, whether civilian or military, was not popular; the opinion of Sgt Irving Shapiro of the 94th Bomb Group being typical:

"The word was around the base that the British food was pretty bad. They put sawdust in their sausages because meat was in short supply. Tasted that way the first and only time I bought sausage and chips in a Bury St Edmunds restaurant."

Despite the general view there were exceptions. Captain Harley Stroven, of 486th Bomb Group at Sudbury, took to something which was not overly popular with the English themselves:

"The bread would arrive at the mess site in GI trucks; the bare loaves unwrapped and lying like so much stove wood, open to the air. But it was good!

I loved that English bread. In my Nissen hut I usually had a loaf. There its texture and flavour reached its peak when toasted over a coke fire, butter melting into its savoury goodness.

The memory of this would be retained, and for years back in Michigan I would tell my family of my love affair with English bread.

I think it was probably as late as the 1970s that I purchased and brought home on a whim a loaf of English muffin bread. It was a new item on our stores shelf. When I bit into that first piece of toast I knew I had found it again."

The standard of menus and cooks varied from mess to mess and even if prepared for Americans by fellow countrymen there could in time be a certain monotony. The tinned pork-based meat loaf Spam tended to feature too often, particularly on toast, where it became vilified as SOS, the OS standing for 'on a slice'.

We carried our fish and chips in a gunny sack in which potatoes had been shipped from America to our base.

Fresh meat and vegetables, coming from British sources, led to mutton and brussel sprouts becoming the major aversions. Brussel sprouts, despite mass objections, continued to feature as a main hot dish vegetable throughout the winter months to become a bad joke. Colonel Stanley Wray, commander of the 91st Bomb Group at Bassingbourn and a delightful humorist, once completed a combat mission briefing session by advising his pilots that if they had to crash on return to England, to do so in a brussel sprouts field.

Some GIs took to a major British refreshment that was not rationed to add variety to their diet. Sgt Roger Armstrong, another Bassingbourn airman:

"At times the men in my bay in the barracks tired of the combat mess hall food. A number of us would decide we wanted fish and chips. One of us would volunteer to ride his bike to Royston, the nearest town. The owner of the fish and chips house would wrap our orders in old newspapers as there was a shortage of wrapping paper and boxes. Fish and chips were the original 'fast food' services in Europe. The chips were more like a steak fried potato, fried in deep fat. The fish was a white fish that was boneless. It was fried in a batter and the two together were very good. On the road back to base I usually found I had a number of English people on bikes following me as I had a light on my bike. There was a shortage of batteries and they were expensive for the local people during the war. We carried our fish and chips in a gunny sack in which potatoes had been shipped from America to our base."

Powdered egg was another common abhorrence and only air crew, in pre-mission breakfast, were served fresh eggs from the limited quantity allocated to each combat station. As every farmer and many house holders in the surrounding countryside kept chickens, off duty egg forays were popular and often rewarding. The base PX (Post Exchange) provided many commodities and articles rationed or scarce in British shops, and as every GI had an entitlement to specified amounts of confectionery, tobacco and toiletries, it was not difficult to find a local who was willing to exchange fresh eggs for such scarcities. Farm eggs were rationed but this did not stop surreptitious transactions. Eggs were not the only potential culinary acquisition in the country-side if one got to know the right people. A pal who was a cook or mess orderly could really enhance such trading and olive drab painted tins of peaches, peanut butter and other delicacies were to be found secreted in country pantries. ■

An introduction to a real American dinner. Major Henry Schlesinger, a Group Surgeon, pours fruit juice for British children at a Thanksgiving Day party, November 1944.

They Don't Speak American Round Here!

A definite profiteer from the American invasion was the taxi business, handicapped only by the petrol rationing. The greatest fear of taxi drivers was damage to their vehicles for frequently a stop to pick up a fare would see the vehicle over-filled by a rush of GIs all wanting to get back to camp. Pleading restrictions on numbers carried usually fell on deaf ears and in the blackout a driver was often not aware of exactly how many passengers were aboard until they left.

A taxi driver in Bedford, having been assured that "there's only six of us aboard Pop" was amazed to see 14 tumble out through the light of a torch shone by an apprehending policeman who had witnessed the mad scramble.

"Not enough petrol" was the taxi driver's best excuse to avoid being hassled, but often the truth. There was one way round fuel shortage as fighter pilot Lt Curtis Smart discovered:

"I had gone to a party in Cambridge and had left late. I was scheduled to fly the next morning and didn't dare miss a combat mission. I got into a taxi and told the driver to take me to Honington. I went to sleep and when the driver woke me and said we had arrived I found we were in Huntingdon! He'd misheard my southern accent. When I told the driver I had to get back to Honington because I had to fly a combat mission, he said he didn't have petrol to get that far - around 40 miles - and he had no coupons to get more. Well, I was not very happy about this. Anyway, he says that Military Officers on vital war business had the right to commandeer taxis in an emergency. Okay, I said, this is an emergency and you are commandeered. He found a garage that had petrol. I signed some kind of paper, and he got the petrol. Fortunately, he got me back to Honington and I flew the mission."

It would be unfair to suggest that many cab drivers were avaricious and overcharged, but there must have been sufficient so inclined for the reputation to have existed. A Royal Navy officer recalls two occasions when he was shunned by taxis in favour of US officer fares and feels this was either due to the expectation of good tips or the possibility of overcharging if his fares did not understand the currency, which was often the case. Daphne Chute, a British woman working for the Americans and wearing her US military uniform, had the experience of being asked a double fare by a taxi driver. Calvin Hill of the 364th Fighter Group was also in no doubt about greedy tendencies:

"On a 'forty-eight' in London, I left a party at around 11.30 pm to go back to my hotel. Found there was a real bad fog, couldn't see your hand in front of your face in the blackout. Asked a taxi driver to take me back to my hotel but he said with the dimmed lights he had he couldn't see which way to go. So I volunteered to lead the way until he could. Started off walking with one foot on the kerb and the other in the gutter. Ended up walking the whole two miles back to my hotel with this taxi following. When we got there the driver wants full fare and I never even got into his cab! ∎

Photo above shows taxis waiting for a fare, Liverpool Street, London. Reproduced by kind permission of The Taxi Museum, London.

"They don't speak American round here - and from what I've heard they don't speak English either" was a well-known quip among GIs who found themselves confronted by the obstacles of the British accent and vernacular.

The United States had its accents but the variations were nowhere near so concentrated as in Britain where it could be notably different in parts of the same county during the early 20th century.

The big troop ships came into the Clyde in Scotland where GIs who had expected no trouble with the language were quickly disillusioned. Arthur Swanson of 357th Fighter Group noted:

"Most GIs were surprised by the great variation in British accents and the fact that some were so heavy they could not understand what was being said. When we docked at Glasgow we were taken by lighter to a railroad station. While the troops waited for a train a woman came along dispensing tea; she kept calling, "Gay yer cunten coups oot" and GIs kept asking each other, "What she say?" Having lived among the Scots community in New York I could translate her request as "Get your canteen cups out.""

Fortunately, most of the USAAF were settled in regions of less extreme dialect but there were still difficulties of communication in rural areas. The publican of an inn at Middleton, Suffolk witnessed an occasion when a friendly GI from the backwoods of Arkansas endeavoured to engage an old farm worker in conversation. It was quickly apparent that they were having difficulty in understanding each other. When the GI had departed, the publican enquired of the local what they had discussed and received the disgruntled "buggered if I know. He din't speak our language". The accent expected was that associated with English characters in the movies, the so-called 'cultivated' accent. Now the GI was to learn that this was associated with the upper classes, BBC announcers or those who aspired to be 'nicely spoken'. This dropping of 'r' and use of a broad 'a' fascinated some American listeners, particularly if it were drawn out to be really plummy.

Misconstrued intentions resulted from some statements. A regular drinker, encountering a GI friend in a pub enquired about the American's usual girlfriend and, on being told "I'm going to have to stand her up" looked about, surprised, and enquired "What, has she had one too many?" Similar ignorance of American expressions resulted in one kind-hearted Hintlesham woman recalling, puzzled, that "Johnny Patton often said he was going to wash up when he'd had a meal with us but he always used to go off to the lavatory and leave us to do it." The significance of 'wash up' never did register with this lady.

Slang was another confusing issue in language. The story is told of two airmen having an argument at the bar of the Lavenham Swan. The barmaid heard one man say to the other, "You want egg in your beer?" and interjected "I'm sorry but I can't do that, eggs are rationed." She was not amused by the mirth engendered until it was explained that 'egg in your beer' meant an unreasonable demand. Many were those natives puzzled by such utterances as "Jus bin shooting the breeze", "I'm gonna hit the sack", "How about cuttin' a rug, babe?" Conversely, Americans delighted in mimicking British wartime slang and colloquialisms: "You've had it!" "You can't miss it!" "Good show!" "Top drawer" "Browned off" "One never knows, does one?" "How's that then?" "I take a dim view" "Actually" "Really" and "Don't you know there's a war on?" being favourites.

British place names were another problem for the visitor as the phonetical pronunciation was frequently wrong. Railway staff and bus conductors had no difficulty when asked, as they frequently were, for "Nor-which", although sometimes the ticket purchaser would insist it said "Nor-which" on his written orders and not "Norridge". They had more trouble sorting out places such as "Dee-bash" and "Whore-ham" as being "Deb-ige" (Debach) and "Horrum" (Horham). ∎

Private Elco Bolton from Florida seeks directions from a bobby, 30 June 1942.

A drive down memory
At prices that will help to take you back.

Hertz advertisement from 1954.

Pictures of English Countryside 1992.

Welcome back.

Hertz UK extends a warm welcome to all those attending the USAAF Reunion celebrations during 1992.

As the official Reunion car hire company, Hertz is offering a special USAAF package of greatly discounted rates, across a wide range of quality rental cars, to everyone participating in the Reunion.

Relive the happy memories in style. Yo will find that travel in a modern Hertz rental car is rather more comfortable th when you were bouncing around in a service jeep fifty years ago.

And, if your memory of the English countryside is the view of fields and ch spires as you flew in and out of your airfield, you can now explore that patchwork of fields and farms by road a leafy lane.

ane with Hertz

MUSTANG — COURTESY OF THE FIGHTER COLLECTION. DUXFORD AIRFIELD

again the picturesque little villages, the
ket towns and country pubs, the
poilt countryside and the beautiful
dy beaches.

p back through the centuries when you
over the old churches and cathedrals,
castles and the stately homes.

enjoy visiting the museums and art
eries, and finding the local crafts and
ques shops. You can see so much more

when you have the freedom of your own
Hertz rental car.

Available from an extensive network of
renting locations at airports and major
towns throughout the country, together
with all the back-up services you might
need whilst on the road. These include free
driving directions using instant
computerised route instructions to help you
plan your journey and free 24 hour AA
emergency road service cover.

*You can take advantage of this special all-
inclusive package, and enjoy all the benefits
of renting from the world's No. 1, by calling
any Hertz reservation centre in the USA, or
upon arrival in the U.K. contact Hertz central
reservations on 081-679 1799 or your local
Mildenhall Hertz branch on 0638 717354
and ask for the USAAF discount rate.*

Have a nice stay!

Photograph reproduced by kind permission of the BT Museum.

During my first trip to London in June or July 1943, my friend Hoffman and I arrived at Liverpool Street Station. We noticed a red phone box on the platform and thought it would be a good idea to phone Rainbow Corner, the servicemen's leisure center at Piccadilly Circus. We wanted to find a bed and breakfast place for the night.

It was during the time when four pennies, the big ones, were required. I knew that much about the phone box, but little more. After I gave the number, having inserted four pence, someone spoke through the receiver saying "Press button "I" (pronounced eye) please". Open-eyed, I spotted "A" and "B", but no "I". I pressed nothing. "I cawn't hear you" she says "Press Button "I"". There is no "I". She thinks I've done it and says "Speak louder please, I cawn't hear you". I do ... she still can't hear me. My friend Hoffman says "Let me get in there. I'll make her hear me". But he had no better luck than me, though he yelled so loudly that many people stared at us. Most everyone was in uniform of some kind.

In disgust, having pressed button "B" to retrieve the four pence, we started walking along the platform. We did not know that in England, some people pronounce "A" like "I"!

Piccadilly Circus, London, during the war years.

And then it happened! An experience I've remembered for over forty-seven years. Not all those platform people were passengers. A man came up to us and said "Say, have you gentlemen been to Petticoat Lane?" "Why, no we haven't" we said. "Today is your lucky day, because I just happen to have the last two tickets to Petticoat Lane" he babbled. "Tell you what, I'll let you have them for half a crown each". I turned to my friend and said "Do you think we ought to go?". "Yes" he says "the last two tickets. Aren't we lucky?" Since this was our first time off base, we didn't know how much half-a-crown was. "Hold out your hand" I said "He will know how much to take". He did. To this day I don't know how much he took, but we were certainly taken.

"Now then" he said "walk up those stairs, turn left and you'll soon see Petticoat Lane".

We did and soon saw what we took to be a marvellous display of merchandise and wares of many shades and varieties. Walking up to a woman stall holder I said "Who collects these tickets?" "What tickets?" I gave them to her and she read "Admit one to Petticoat Lane. You've been had. No one has to pay to walk down this street".

But it never happened a second time. On the contrary, we found the people very helpful, warm and courteous. ■

Jim Johnson, who was based at Horham

The Imperial War Museum welcomes USAAF veterans to London

Imperial War Museum

Voted Museum of the Year 1990

The museum of twentieth century warfare, includes displays on the Second World War

Blitz Experience - a dramatic recreation of what it was like to live through an air raid

See the P51D Mustang, the Churchill tank and a Supermarine Spitfire

Open daily 10.00am - 6.00pm

Cabinet War Rooms

The underground headquarters provided to protect Churchill and his War Cabinet against air raids in the Second World War

See the Transatlantic Telephone Room from which Churchill could speak to President Roosevelt in the White House.

Free sound guide

Near Westminster and the Houses of Parliament

Open daily 10.00am - 6.00pm (last admission 5.15pm)

HMS Belfast

Visit Europe's largest surviving Second World War warship, that helped sink the Scharnhorst, and saw action on D-Day

Seven decks to explore from the Bridge to the Boiler and Engine Rooms

Now moored in the Thames near the Tower of London

Open daily 10.00am - 6.00pm

FOR FURTHER INFORMATION ON ALL SITES TELEPHONE 071-416 5000

It was November, 1943 and a very foggy night. The occasion was one of my first visits to London and we were returning on the train. The word 'Bovril' appeared at one of the stations. Nothing else was on the sign. Another GI said to me "It's a bad fog, really bad, he's going round in a circle. We've been through Bovril twice before!"

We did not know, being foreigners, that Bovril was a drink!

Jim Johnson

A 1940s advertisement for Bovril. Reproduced by kind permission of CPC (United Kingdom) Ltd.

Somewhere in England ...

To make the most of the limited trans-Atlantic airmail, a special letter form was available to US servicemen. Microfilmed V-Mail negative on a reel carried hundreds of these letters to the USA where they were enlarged and sent to the addresses at no cost to the sender. Reproduced here at actual size is Sgt Robert Sand's first letter to his parents. 'Somewhere in England', in this case, was Nuthampstead.

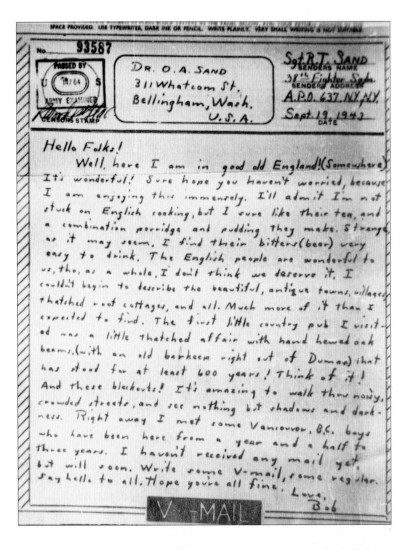

Technical Sergeant Alfred L Lieberman of Long Island, NY relaxes on his bed at an American Army Air Force station at Molesworth, with a copy of the special newspaper produced for American troops in Britain.

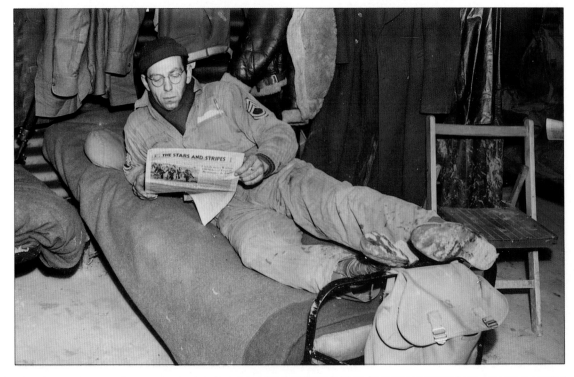

It is hardly a drawing room tea party, but Sgt Sam E Frisella finds it quite a comfortable way to keep his feet out of the mud while drinking his tea and reading a letter from home at an American Air Corps station in England.

Dear Family

I'm sorry I can't tell you ... when we first arrived, how we travelled and where we are. However, I can say that England is really beautiful - everything is so neat and orderly. The trains are just like in the movies - only no sleeping accommodations except luxury trains, no dining cars. Sunday we visited Cambridge which is quaint - no buildings are over 3 storeys. The streets are cobblestone and run in every damned direction! The lower class English rather resent us, however, the middle class and upper bend over backwards being nice to us.

We are at one of the finest Airdromes; the accommodations are excellent. In fact they beat those of my former station. Virginia creeper, ivy and honeysuckle grow on many of the structures and there are lawns, roses and poplars. A few observations on the customs. We're taking to 'tea' wonderfully ... the Bank of England (Lloyds?) representative changed our money. I can't make change yet, they have a god awful system.

The Scotch people we have met are really swell, more like Yanks.

We have to watch our slang. Have already had a few misunderstandings that way.

The British version of toilet tissue is equivalent to the rotogravure section of the Sears Roebuck catalogue. There are no oranges. We will soon be eating American food tho' I like English food, but they have tried to cook our dishes and have flopped so far. But their hospitality extended that far!

The English people have taken a terrible beating in the air raids and many people show it. When they play they play hard, though they have very high spirits and rarely speak of the war except in passing, or else of the end of it. They have no doubts as to an English victory.

The British WAAFs (Womens Army Air Force) are taken very seriously, and do a good job. We palled up with a few at a pub and they knew our latest songs and some slang ... the English seem to feel that our high pay will buy up everything in the way of luxuries; one British Major said to me that if we kept drinking at the rate we were (really very little on American standards) all the Scotch in England would be gone in a month! So you can see, we are rightly called 'crazy Yanks' (they call us Yanks whatever we are).

The blackouts are terrific, 100% all over. I've bumped into lamp posts a hundred times and said politely 'beg your pardon'.

In conclusion, I'm well, I'm happy ... I like the country, the people and a fraction of the customs.

A letter sent home by Sam G Wilson, 2nd Lt, 17th Bomb Group, 34th Bomb Squadron, upon his arrival in England, October 1942.

If you send a package make it the size of a shoe box. I'd like some pine nuts, stamps and airmail stationery. I'll write soon again.

All my love Sam.

The Mission

No rest for the mechanics! The hangar crew work all night on a reluctant engine.

Preparations for a combat bombing mission at a bomber airfield began during the night, with operations and intelligence staff producing the necessary flight plans and target information for pilots, navigators and bombardiers, and issuing details of fuel and bomb loads to the maintenance and ordnance sections. The personnel of combat crews would be awakened about three hours before the scheduled take-off time, going first to breakfast and then to the briefing for the mission. Heavy sheepskin and electrically heated flying suits were donned before the crews were transported out to the aircraft.

Mechanics had been pre-flighting their aircraft for several hours before the combat crews arrived, sometimes for most of the night - and they did not eat or sleep until the aircraft had departed. At the pre-arranged time, engines would be started and the bombers moved out from their dispersal points onto the airfield perimeter track. Departure was a noisy business with perhaps 25 aircraft - and in later years near double that number - lined one behind the other on the track, waiting turn to take off. Each

had four 1,200 hp engines running, opened up to full power for take-off. A fully laden Fortress or Liberator required all of a 4,500 ft runway and most of a 6,000 ft runway to obtain the desired speed for a good lift-off - about 120 mph. It was an apprehensive time for the crews for they knew that if an engine failed as they left

They knew that if an engine failed as they left the ground, the chances were that the bomber would abruptly return to earth.

the ground, the chances were that the bomber would abruptly return to earth and crashing with bombs and 2,800 gallons of fuel meant an explosion and fire. There was not an 8th Air Force heavy bomber base that did not experience a fatal take-off crash and at most there were several during the course of operations.

The bombers took off at 30-45 second intervals, climbed steadily away from the airfield to a specified area of sky where they orbited while

A group of fighter pilots leaving the parachute room at Metfield to board the jeeps which will take them to the flight line.

gaining altitude. Aircraft following the leader would shorten their turns so that gradually a formation was assembled: first flights then squadrons and finally group formations of up to 27 aircraft in the early days, but with 36 or more in later months. It took about two hours to assemble and marshal formations and to reach the required altitude, generally about 20,000 ft, for striking out for the sea and enemy territory. The height was necessary to minimize the effects of enemy anti-aircraft fire (flak) on crossing the enemy held coastline.

On clear days the morning departures provided the most extraordinary sight as, often, hundreds of bombers curved through the heavens, their paths marked by the white streaks of vapour trails that quickly expanded into broad bends. The hot engine exhaust mixing with the frigid air at high altitude produced the vapour which in some weather conditions actually persisted to produce an overcast. The aircraft within a squadron formation were staggered up and down and from side to side, while the three squadrons that usually composed a group formation were similarly staggered so that the whole resembled an angled wedge. The object was to give clear fields of fire to as many gun positions as possible and minimise the risk of gunners actually shooting into other bombers in the formation.

Two, three or four groups eventually positioned relative to one another to form a Combat Wing and Combat Wings, separated by a few miles, sallied forth in trail to complete the Divisional Air Task Force. At the appointed time, known as Zero Hour, the force headed out over a prominent landmark, usually a town, on the English coast. Planning times for the mission were all worked out both back and forth from Zero Hour. The duration of the mission obviously depended on the distance to be flown and while an attack on the Ruhr might take only six hours overall, many distant

At the appointed time, known as Zero Hour, the force headed out over a prominent landmark.

targets demanded flight times of 10 or 11 hours before the returning bombers landed at base. Once the enemy coast had been re-crossed on withdrawal, formations reduced altitude so that the crews could come off oxygen and to allow the formation to spread out to ease pilots' concentration on keeping close station. When regaining England, the Fortresses and Liberators were down to a few thousand feet and often swept over the countryside towards their bases at not far above church steeple height. The formation was retained until reaching the vicinity of the home base, when

B-24 Liberators from the 93rd Bomb Group in practice formation over Norfolk, June 1943.

squadrons would separate and orbit while the aircraft in each 'peeled off' to make a landing approach. Bombers firing two red flares indicated wounded on board and a request for priority to come in first. Often battle damaged - ragged tail planes, holed wings, feathered (stationary) propellers - were clearly visible to people in the vicinity of an airfield as the bombers returned.

Trucks would pick up the crews at the aircraft dispersal points and take them to the interrogation building. Here, while the men ate doughnuts and drank coffee, intelligence officers would take down details of what befell and what was seen by each crew. After interrogation the men were free to return to their barracks. Even though young - average age of 22 - most were exhausted. The reduced air pressure experienced in high altitude flight made digestive systems uneasy and induced fatigue. Added to this, the constant noise - only partially subdued by earphones - the extreme cold, discomfort of wearing an oxygen mask, to say nothing of apprehension and fear, put considerable strain on the strongest of constitutions. As a result many combat men spent much of their non-flying time sleeping. Extreme tiredness was a common post-mission experience. ■

Pilots' flying helmets, oxygen masks, ear phones and flight jackets hang ready for use.

Members of a 401st Bomb Group combat crew are interrogated at their Deenethorpe base, after a bombing mission. Note whiskey bottle to aid relaxation - every man could have a measure from this on return from a mission.

Big Dip for Big Shorty

'Hottest tail in town'. Checking his tail guns in last minute readiness. S/Sgt Joseph F Kotlarz reigns over the tail gun position in the Fortress, 'Kipling's Error III' which is ready to be despatched on a combat mission.

On August 25, 1944, the B-17G known as 'Big Shorty' thundered into the air at 0825 hours, climbed to altitude and took her place in the formation of the 447th Bomb Group. The crew consisted of Pilot Lt Eldon 'Bud' Henningsen; Co-pilot Lt Henry R Manual; Navigator Lt Arnold 'Wally' Wallstrom; Bombadier Lt Charles B McGuire; Ft Engineer Sgt Otis O Lumpkin; Radio Operator Sgt John Kates; Waist Gunner Sgt Lee B Plant; Ball Turret Gunner Sgt William Holloman and Tail Gunner Sgt Harry Long.

Laden with bombs and a full gas load, Big Shorty was set for a long haul. At briefing that morning we were informed that this mission, while a long one, was practically a milk run since there were only sixteen anti-aircraft guns at the target, which was the experimental rocket works at Rechlin, Germany. This was the installation where Werner von Braun was building the V-2 rockets with which the Germans where then blasting London.

Since we were a relatively new crew our position was almost in the middle of the formation. We by-passed the target to the north, made a huge right turn and struck from 25,000 feet headed back west. Perhaps five or ten seconds after bombs away, there was a sudden shuddering impact which caused the ship to heel dangerously to the right. With all his strength, Bud fought the controls until we were back in position, but smoke and fire were streaming from under number one engine, while the propellor hung at a crazy angle. Another heavy thud indicated another hit, this one just under number four engine which instantly showed a serious loss of power. By now, we were sliding

The third impact struck the tail section and shook the ship like a dog shakes a bone.

backwards out of the formation. The third impact struck the tail section and shook the ship like a dog shakes a bone. The fourth and last one seemed to be in the bomb bay area and ripped huge holes in the central section of the ship. We had flown precisely down the track of a four gun battery.

At this point we were out of formation, number one engine dead and on fire, part of the rudder shot away, the elevators damaged, bomb bay riddled and number four engine showing distressing signs of power failure. To put it mildly, the ship was a mess. Fortunately, the shell that struck number one engine was a dud and did not explode, but the fire it started was our primary problem at the time. Bud signalled me to get on the controls with him

and we proceeded to put the ship into a side-slip to the right, dropping about four thousand feet. It worked. The fire was blown out and did not start again. The wind-milling prop was a problem, also, but try as we might, we could not shake it off.

Lt Wallstrom came on the intercom and stated that Sweden was only about 120 miles away and I asked him for a heading. He gave it and I relayed this message to Bud, but he said we must remember that there was no air-sea rescue in the Baltic Sea, and if we had to bail out we wouldn't live but a minute or two in that water. It was his suggestion that we head west

We scattered machine guns, spare parachutes and everything else the gunners could pull or chop loose, all the way across Denmark.

across Denmark towards England. We didn't know at this time that we had sizeable holes shot in two or more gas tanks. Bud took over the controls and asked if anyone had been wounded or injured. I had Sgt Lumpkin check and he came back with the welcome news that everyone was quite all right. There was, however, a problem. Sgt Holloman was trapped in the ball turret and couldn't rotate it far enough to get the door open due to damage from flak having struck one of the gears. I called Holly on the intercom to ask how he was doing. He informed me that he was fine and stated that we should do whatever was necessary to protect ourselves and the rest of the crew. I found out later that he believed at this time that we were going to have to bail out and leave him. Part of the intercom had been damaged and Holly's voice was blurred and indistinct, which prompted me to ask him where he got that mouth full of mush he was speaking through. His answer was a classic "Sir, that's not mush, that's fingernails". I asked 'Tex' Lumpkin to go back and make every effort to get Holly out of that turret and he left the flight deck.

Bud issued an order that all extra weight be tossed overboard. We scattered machine guns, ammunition, flak suits, spare parachutes and everything else the gunners could pull or chop loose, all the way across Denmark. Sgt Plant was reluctant to let go of his guns and ammo, but when I informed him that he had to, he brought them forward and dropped them from the bomb bay, watched the last belt of ammo fall, turned and stepped back into the radio room and slammed the door. A few seconds later, the tail section of the ship lurched to the left and Bud fought the controls until she was on course once more, but almost instantly the same thing happened again. We looked at each other and shrugged our shoulders. The same thing happened two or three times more and it wasn't until we were down in the life rafts that we solved the mystery. Harry Long was telling that he had to sit crosswise in the tail section and brace his feet against the escape hatch to force it open far enough to get rid of his guns and ammo.

Just prior to this, number four engine made a rattling, growling noise and quit running, but Bud reached over and punched the feathering button and lo and behold it worked. The huge propellor slowly twisted into the wind and stopped spinning.

However, Wally and I decided that we had better check the gas consumption if we could, so I read the gauges and fed him the information. A few seconds went by and Wally yelled

Lower and lower she sank until ..... she slipped beneath the surface and was gone forever.

into the intercom that something was very wrong, either the information I gave him wasn't right or we had burned just about twice the amount of gas that we should have. We checked again but, alas, the figures seemed to be correct, so now we knew that there was no chance of reaching England.

Number two engine picked this time to make a powerful hissing sound and as we

someone mentioned about Harry pulling the handles and he said "Yeah, I broke 'em both off!" I nicknamed him 'Harry the Horse'.

'Tex' came through the bulkhead door and reported that Holly was out of the ball turret. This was the best news that Bud and I had had in several hours.

At approximately 1625 hours, with all the crew except Bud and I in the radio room, we set Big Shorty down in the North Sea about thirty miles from the coast of Holland. The landing was a classic, due mainly to the absolute perfection of Lt Henningsen's flying skill. It was for this feat that he was awarded his first Distinguished Flying Cross. Big Shorty floated serenely on the heavy swells for thirty-six minutes giving us more than ample time to get out. Slowly, the nose sank deeper until at last she tipped straight up on her nose with about twenty feet of the tail section out of the water. Lower and lower she sank until, with a gurgle of bubbles and leaving a small oil slick, she slipped beneath the surface and was gone forever.

Bud and I were so sea-sick in those life rafts that we would have had to get better before we could have died. At one point during the two hours that we were out there, we found ourselves looking each other in the face and Bud grinned a very sickly grin and said "Bob, it looks like it's going to be a damned long war". I had to agree; this was my third mission and Bud's fifth.

An Air Sea Rescue P-47 showed up and stayed with us until the boat got to us. He dropped us a nice, dry dinghy and some smoke bombs to guide the boat to us.

A B-17 Flying Fortress over the A120, just west of Great Dunmow, Essex.

looked a stream of oil as thick as my thumb shot from under the cowl and up over the wing. I poked the feathering button and the engine went dead. Left with one engine and losing just about 150 feet a minute of altitude, there was no alternative - we would have to ditch.

Before we ditched I talked to Harry Long and asked him to take the responsibility of pulling the two red handles in the radio room that would release our life rafts when we stopped in the water. After we got into the rafts

The next day, after returning to our own base, Bud and I had to go to the intelligence office to file our combat reports. It was then that the intelligence officer told us that there was a high school in the area of the target and when there was an air raid the students manned the anti-aircraft guns. This was bad enough, but as we were leaving the office he said "Fellows, it's a girls' school". We never lived it down. ■

Henry R Manuel

Little Mac

"When we lasted long enough they gave us medals; when we died they said "Our casualties were low""
Randall Jarrell

We often forget that it took ten combat air crew members to put a heavy bomber into the fray; the men who flew the B-17 Flying Fortress on missions into Europe - remember that 60 per cent of the fighting and dying was done by the crews' enlisted aerial gunners. This is the true story of one such airman, S/Sgt George B McLaughlin, a ball turret gunner with the 535th bombardment squadron, 381st Bombardment Group, Ridgewell aerodrome, Essex.

During the dark days of the winter of 1943/44, I had the opportunity to meet and know a lot of outstanding ball turret gunners and I remember Ken Stone in the 532nd Sqdn, Ed 'Shortround' Gartland with the 534th, John M 'Shorty' Howery, John Woods and 'Little Mac', all of the 535th. I envied all of these ball turret gunners, as they could all fit into the power turret while wearing their parachutes. If their aircraft was hit, they had only to trip the hatch latches and roll into the slipstream. I was 6 feet tall and felt lucky to get into the turret while wearing a chest pack harness alone. This meant in case of a bail out I had to get out of the

turret, back up into the fuselage to clip on my parachute pack. When we attended specialised briefings I remember hearing remarks like 'Here comes O'Brien and his leprechauns' or 'Glory be, it's Legs O'Brien and the wee people'.

I had first met George McLaughlin after the second Schweinfurt 'Black Thursday' raid of 14th October, 1943. Little Mac was already a tested veteran of the air war. This was his mission number eleven and my mission number

"You're going to be all right lad, let me show you some tricks of the trade".

three. It was my feeling at this point in time, I would never be able to complete a tour of combat and return home again. Thankfully Little Mac took me under his wing after this mission. "You're going to be all right lad, let me show you some tricks of the trade".

He was true to his word and he gave freely of his time. He taught me how to slot a cover plate of a .50 caliber aircraft machine gun so you

This photograph, taken early morning, 14th July 1943, shows vapour trails made by a large force of Fortresses, flying in tight formation as they passed over a south London suburb.

could clear a feeding malfunction while in the turret. We took two loops off the range input spring under the foot pedal, which permitted the target easy and smooth on tracking. Then he arranged a trade with an RAF gunner in the 90th Squadron at Mildenhall for a pair of RAF flying boots. The heel just fit into the target range pedal and the hard soles would permit you to walk out if you survived a bail out. He advised me to get rid of the link chutes as at

He was already an old man to me, he was 27 when I came into life.

certain clock positions of the turret, the slip-stream would twist the links and jam the weapon. "Don't worry about the dam links O'Bie, let them free fall into the turret - you can drop them out after the fighters leave you". I have always followed his recommendation to load the guns hot. To hand charge at least five rounds through each turn, to check the feeding and to ensure the chambering of a live round. I learned to dry the firing pin springs with a pipe cleaner and to carry two electric extension cords for my heated suit. One was preset in the turret with the heat rehostat pre-adjusted under the gunner's seat. I also added to my equipment an empty nose-fuse can from a 500 pound bomb. This was used as a relief container for nature's call, without leaving the turret. The Mac showed me how to enter a little elevation creep into the turret drive system. "Now if you are hit and/or unconscious the guns will depress to 90 degrees and the waist gunner or radio operator can open the turret door and extract you." The final lesson he passed on to me was this - "O'Bie, always keep a set of your own bolt studs. You will play hell trying to find a pair before a mission". He then presented me with a pair of ball turret charging bolt studs with welded on eyelets so I could secure them on my person with a clip-on key chain.

In addition to these noted lessons of survival, Little Mac taught me what it means to be human. He was already an old man to me, he was 27 when I came into life, but most important he was an educated man and had completed studies at the graduate level. We had many enlightening talks together and on some days I travelled with him to visit in the University libraries at Cambridge. I was dumbfounded one day when he asked me if I knew what I was fighting for and I replied "personal survival".

He was quiet for a moment and then said "O'Bie, I know what you say is true, but do you realise that something much more important than your personal safety is being contested. Do you know what that is?"

B-17 Fortresses of the 381st Bomb Group in the morning mist at Ridgewell.

When I admitted that I didn't understand his meaning, he told me the story of Thermopylae (480 BC) and about Leonidas and the Spartans' last stand. This was a struggle between barbarianism and civilisation and he explained how such a conflict is more important than the individuals involved, for it is the struggle between savagery and reason. I have thought about his lesson many times since then - the eternal conflict between night and day and good and evil.

We kept plugging away, flying the missions as they came up until the raid of 20th December, 1943 at Bremen. Our squadron was hard hit and Little Mac's heated suit had shorted out. He had suffered third degree frost bite and had to be evacuated to the general hospital at Ely. I was able to check out a jeep and went to visit with him over the Christmas holidays. At this time he reminded me once again "O'Bie, be sure you examine your beliefs very carefully. Remember that if something is not worth living for, it is certainly not worth dying for". Now before Little Mac was returned

to flying duties, his crew was missing in action at Oschersleben, Germany on 11th January 1944. Upon his return to the unit he was assigned as a spare ball turret gunner and moved into a hut that housed the spare crew members. We called these quarters the 'Leper Colony'. By mid-March Mac had completed five more missions, including the first three Berlin raids on 6th, 8th and 9th March, 1944. Luck was riding with him and it looked as if he would complete his tour soon and return to his home in Doylestown, PA.

At long last we worked out a deal with the orderly room that permitted Little Mac to move into our hut. It was a pleasure to have him as our guest while he awaited the call for his last mission. I shall always remember the many happy hours we spent in discussion. Mac was so well versed in the classics that the hours just flew by. Little Mac was a deeply religious man and he read silently from his bible every evening before retiring. The unit had flown an easy mission to Brussels, Belgium. This was number 24 for Little Mac - just one more to go and he was home safe.

We knew that a mission was scheduled for the next day. As the Liberty run had been cancelled, and Mac would be flying number 25 with one of our newer crews. I shall never forget that night before Mac's last mission. He had been reading from his bible and he laid the book down and said "O'Bie, are you awake?". "Ya, Mac, what is it compadre?". He sat silent for a few moments then said "O'Bie, I will never go home again".

There was no trace of fear in his voice, no panic, it was just a statement as a matter of fact, with calm acceptance.

"But Mac, you only have one to go, you are going home to Doylestown and you are going to get that long black limousine. It's going to be so long that you will need an interphone to talk with the driver and it will have to have hinges to negotiate corners. You will wear a big red carnation in your lapel and carry a gold tipped walking cane and all of the good citizens of

Doylestown are going to look in wonder and say "There goes Mr Mac. He was a BTO in the ETO".

"No, O'Bie. I know it will all end here. Promise me that you will do some things for me".

He gave me three sealed letters to be mailed and a list of his personal possessions and the names of those he wished to receive them. Then

"Remember that if something is not worth living for, it is certainly not worth dying for".

he reached into the side pocket of his B-4 bag and handed me 8 bolt studs for the ball turret guns.

We had breakfast together the next morning, picked up our personal equipment and went to the aircraft - loaded and waiting. I was sure wrong about one thing. This was not to be a milk run, our targets were located at Cottbus and Sorau, all the way to the Polish frontier. We started engines and taxied on time. Little Mac's aircraft 'Piccadilly Tilly II' was three ahead of us in take off order. The tower fired the green flare and the launch was on. Then something happened to 'Tilly'. The no 3 engine exploded right after lift-off. The aircraft burst into flame, made a violent turn to the right, turned upside down and impacted about three miles from the station. It was a blazing inferno, no survivors.

The crews' remains were interred in the American Military cemetery at Cambridge, in a common grave with a single grave marker.

In April 1957, while my SAC unit was deployed to Mildenhall with a tanker task force, I took the opportunity to visit Madingley and pay my last respects to Little Mac.

Somehow I am sure that Mac knew that I had returned, to give testimony, and that I was going to tell the lacedaemonians that here, obedient to their laws, you fell. ∎

Tom O'Brien

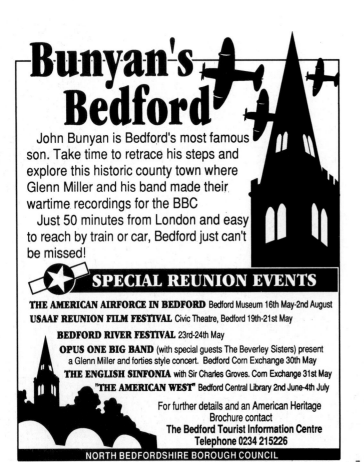
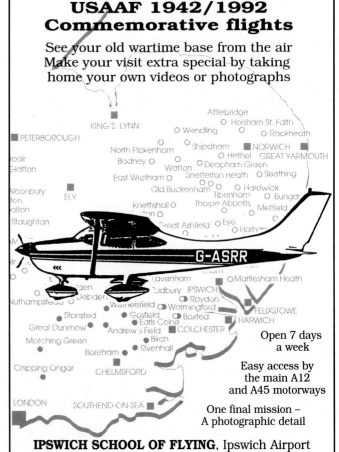

Para-pup!

The pedigree mongrel, complete with dog tags on his collar, checks that the parachute packers do their job correctly.

At Andrews Field it was reported that there was a one year old Lieutenant who ate in the Officers' Mess hall and flew combat missions in a B-26!

After investigation this would appear to be true. Second Lieutenant Salvo, service number 0-000000 and 'assistant bombadier' to Lieutenant Fletcher was such an age, but was not much of a man. He was a one year old fox terrier who just wouldn't be parted from his master and his master's friends and stood in front of their aircraft's wheels before take-off. The only way to quieten him was to haul him aboard and continue. Officially these flights were for training purposes only, but it is recorded that two combat missions were made.

In case of trouble, Salvo had been 'issued' with a parachute and life vest, made from surplus material, as well as the obligatory 'dog tags'! To test the parachute, classified as experimental, Salvo was jettisoned several times over the base and, according to contemporary residents of Great Saling, enjoyed the events greatly, barking and wagging his tail all the way down and, on landing, rolling over and running towards his master's aircraft when it touched down. He could always tell the correct machine from all the others with the same olive drab paint. ∎

Salvo's parachute harness provided a handy carrying handle when his befrienders, the crew of the 452nd Bomb Squadron Marauder 'Jezabelle' helped the dog aboard for a flight.

Yesterday's Witness

On this particular morning Walter was on his 1920 Coventry Eagle motor cycle. The 850 cc JAP sloping twin engine had a kick like a mule and needed careful management of the decompression lever. In frost and mud it was impossible to hold the machine upright and it was with a sense of achievement that Walter left it in the Souldrop Wold barns, both he and it in one piece.

Life at Colworth had been transformed by the war with Germany, even though it was remote from the main target areas of the Luftwaffe. But nothing made as much impact as the military aerodrome at Podington. When

shrouded airfield for over a week. As Walter Nottage began his journey to Hinwick he was conscious of two things. First, there was little or no improvement in the weather, secondly by the roar of the unsilenced aircraft engines it was evident that some desperately important mission had persuaded the base commander, Colonel James Wilson to order his crews to fly. The B-17 Flying Fortresses were already thundering down the runway at 90 second intervals. An all instrument take-off was possible, but because of the narrow runway, most pilots would not trust the gyrocompass. Waver a fraction of a degree and the bomber would cartwheel into oblivion, its payload of

It was a bitterly cold December, in fact the coldest for 54 years. Colworth was blanketed with fog, the twigs of every tree and shrub white with its frozen crystals since the middle of the month. On December 24th Walter Nottage, Lord Melchett's gamekeeper's son, delayed his journey from Windmill Hill Cottage to Hinwick Lodge Farm until well after daybreak. Then about 24 years old, he was working as a tractor driver and walked or travelled by motorcycle the mile or so, crossing the 'Forty Foot' unclassified County Highway on his way to Hinwick Lodge.

Command and staff of the 92BG, October 1944. Lt Col James W Wilson is fifth from the left.

built in 1942 its eastern boundary just brushed the northern tip of Colworth Estate, one mile as the crow flies from Colworth House itself. Podington aerodrome had become an operational base for the 92nd Bombardment Group.

The war in Europe was at a critical stage and frequently the base sent out its Fortresses in daily succession. However, by the 24th December, 1944, not a plane had left the fog

six 1,000 bombs and 2,780 gallons of fuel guaranteeing a spectacular finish. One runway light at a time was now visible and the mist was patchy rather than dense. Six hundred yards from the end of the runway the air corridor was one hundred yards wide, with Souldrop barns to the south and Great Hayes Wood to the north. The bombers were still so low that they could almost 'be touched with a broomstick'.

As Walter neared the forty foot track which hugged the south side of Great Hayes, he moved under the flight path and now had the comfort of knowing he was distancing himself from the noise and danger.

Then Walter heard the roar of a B-17 engine on a flight path which would pass in front of him. Watching it appear through the broken mist he saw the pilot bearing north in a desperate attempt to avoid the wood. The crew of B-17 G.30 DL-42-38101 had arrived at Podington base on 16th December and had never seen the airfield or its surroundings except wrapped in a blanket of fog. This was the crew's first mission and the pilot, 2nd Lt Robert Seeber was well aware of his awesome responsbility. The B-17 was failing to develop sufficient power to climb significantly and as the plane banked, it encountered the propwash of the aircraft in front which caused it to lose control and lose altitude.

As the B-17's collision became inevitable, Walter's mind moved into top gear. He was witnessing a developing tragedy which would engulf the crew of nine and, if he moved nearer, could extinguish his own life in a split second. The bomber struck the top of the trees, its dipping left wing driving into the wood. The engine propellers on full thrust sheared and the fifty foot long wing structure disintegrated. A spar from the splintered framework spun through the air travelling over a hundred yards, one end driving into the ground, the remaining thirty feet projecting vertically like a newly erected aerial.

The main body of the plane driven by the right side engines plunged into Great Hayes Wood. The bulk of the fuselage was shattered, but it was right side up. There is little doubt that already some of the crew were dead or mortally injured.

The mechanics of the crash were not a consideration of Walter Nottage, as he ran to the point where the main body of the plane had plunged into the woods. The fuel tanks in the wings fractured and within seconds the heat of the engines ignited a series of fires along the path of the stricken bomber. Making his way to the shattered fuselage Walter moved immediately to one of the gaping holes. He found Sgt William Brockmeyer, the engineer, with a badly injured foot, his right hand fingers sheared off at the first joint. He, the pilot and co-pilot, owed survival of the impact to their location on top of the aircraft's main body in the strong centre part. Walter returned twice more to the plane, rescuing the pilot and co-pilot, 2nd Lts Robert Seeber and William McQuinn. He half pulled, half carried, the badly shocked men to a safe distance in the trees where, watching the fire increase in intensity, they endured the bitter realisation that there was no hope of res-cue for the rest of the crew. The heat melted the aluminium skin, which buckled and sagged, exposing the skeleton framework of the air-craft. Now the outline of the 1000 pound bombs could be seen, like the eggs of a malevolent phoenix waiting for the moment when the developing inferno would complete their incu-bation. The tremendous explosion which followed destroyed all that was recognisable as an aircraft. It was half an hour before the crash tender and ambulances arrived from the base, picking their way through a track gouged through the hedgerows some months earlier by a crashed B-24 Liberator.

The remaining B-17s continued to take off, aware of the red glow which penetrated the fog. They joined formation and began the long

Of the fifty one bombers that left Podington, only thirteen made it back to the base that night.

climb across the Channel to their destination, Giessen airfield. Of the fifty one bombers that left Podington, only thirteen made it back to the base that night. Six crashed, seventeen airmen were known to be dead, nine missing and many injured. Fog closed the airfield by mid-afternoon and most of the 92nd Group landed near Bury St Edmunds. For the 92nd it was the most disastrous day since the September 1944 raids on the oil refineries at Werseberg.

A few months later Walter Nottage was officially commended for his great courage in a letter from Colonel James Wilson, the Podington base commander. This was followed by a commendation from King George VI. He was awarded the British Empire Medal for Gallantry "for heroic acts in saving the lives of three airmen from a burning aircraft. Had it not been for your gallant disregard for your own personal safety, these Army Air Force airmen would have perished in the burning aircraft and ensuing bomb explosion."

Walter and his wife Eileen now live quietly at Odell, but his courage founded a lifetime friendship with the rescued men and has prompted several transatlantic visits. The epic event in a Bedfordshire woodland may be painful to remember, but it is impossible to forget. ■

Mike Jones

Crew of the A-20 Havoc 'Angel II'. Left to right: Chester Dunaj, Earl Bever and Fred Yoos who were lost over Brest in September 1944. Kneeling is William Dorward, the ground crew chief.

Remembered are the many kindnesses and acts of sharing that helped ease the War experience, like when you and your co-gunner Andy returned from a 48 hour pass to London and someone in the 645th Motor Pool - you still don't know who, but God bless them for their thoughtfulness - met you at Chelmsford with an Army ambulance, parked next to the truck sent to take the 410th Bomb Group men back to Gosfield. Just as you were about to climb up the truck tailgate, the ambulance driver and his buddy called out "Andy and Spider, hop into the back of the ambulance, where you can rest on the cots". Eagerly you climbed inside and shouted insults to those who had to ride the truck while you went first-class. Only after the rear doors were shut did the two 645th Motor Pool men turn in their compartment and quietly say "We lost Dunaj and Yoos yesterday, we're very sorry fellers". They were not following any prescribed military procedure; they had merely anticipated the shock you would undergo at this news and the need for a bit of privacy en route back to the field. Days later, you realised that they had used the word 'We', not 'You lost Dunaj and Yoos', but 'We' did. That's what made the 410th the best damn Bomb Group in the world.

Edward D Dionne, 410BG, 645BS

A Happy Ending

An American bomber crew rescued from 'the drink' by RAF Air Sea Rescue.

I was one of the original pilots of the 351st Bomb Group that flew over in April 1943 and wound up at Polebrook. Most of us would have happily changed places with anyone else that summer ... anyone, that is, except the RAF bomber crews who, to our absolute amazement, went out at night. A natural bond formed between us when we learned to our surprise that they felt the same way about our daylight bombing.

On 17 July, 1943 returning from a mission to Hannover (my thirteenth), our plane, 'Snowball', caught the brunt of a head-on attack. After a twenty minute air battle I ditched the plane in the North Sea, midway between Amsterdam and England. The nine of us who survived to climb into liferafts were later found by the pilot of an Anson, picked up by the crews of two Walruses and transferred to two naval launches. Three hours and several bottles of Johnny Walker later, we staggered happily onto the wharf at Great Yarmouth, more inebriated than hurt. Ambulances took us to a Roman Catholic hospital in town, where we spent the night. The last thing we wanted to see the next morning was fish, but at breakfast we were confronted by kippers!

A week or so later, I was called to London for a live radio interview by a correspondent of CBS News. There, for the first time, I met Pilot Officer John Clark of Edinburgh, the skipper of an RAF Air-Sea Rescue launch at Great Yarmouth. Our helpful correspondent introduced us and handed us scripts. As Clark and I soon discovered, they recounted his totally-imagined story of my rescue by Clark. Our first reaction was to return to our bases; our second, to rewrite the script. I had a secret reason for wanting to appear. My wife was a month short of having our first child and I hoped that hear-

ing my voice would be an antidote for the fright she must have suffered when she learned that we had been shot down.

So we rewrote the script, corrected its many factual errors and turned the program into honest interviews with the pilot of a rescued crew and the RAF skipper of a rescue launch. The final outcome was a compromise; the correspondent insisted on maintaining the fiction that Clark had rescued us, but that false story now had at least the virtue of sounding possible. Just before the broadcast, in the bowels of the BBC, I met Edward R Murrow, who had just completed his justly famous 'This is London ...' report for that night.

My hunch about my wife's reaction turned out to be accurate; a New York producer told me on the air after the broadcast that she had just given birth to a baby girl and that both were well. I learned later that my premature daughter's birth was announced at the end of the program over the entire CBS radio network. Years later, when I interviewed Ed Murrow for a magazine article, I told him about his fellow CBS newsman's falsification of the news and he was properly appalled. ■

William Peters, Connecticut

We all looked alike. We bragged because we were scared. We knew you tolerated us and since I was late arriving it was easier for me. Many of your countrymen got to know some of the crews and when they didn't return I suppose there were some regrets ... I think you got to love us in a way. In the movie 'Memphis Belle' one gunner read a poem that is so true. He wrote words to this effect: "There was nothing before and there shall be nothing again but this moment together". So true.

John Russell, Florida

A Memorable Christmas

Everything was coated with hoar frost, an extraordinary spectacle. John Knipe pauses for a buddy to take a photo while on his way to the mess hall at Raydon airfield.

Christmas 1944 brought sadness to the 94th Bomb Group. There was more despair than hope. It was one of the very worst winters on record in England for heavy snows and ice, not only that, heavy fog blanketed the base at Bury St Edmunds airfield, Rougham, so that pilots, incoming from missions, some on damaged aircraft and almost out of fuel, had to strain every nerve and every skill they knew to attempt a safe landing on runways they could not see.

On 24th December over 2,000 Fortresses and Liberators, with a massive fighter escort departed England in clear skies to make up for lost time. The target was Babenhouser, Germany marshalling yards.

As they approached Rougham on their return to base a heavy fog obscured it. Rougham was the only safe haven base open and was compelled to receive many other returning planes from other bases. This meant 150 aircraft had to be accommodated in space normally allocated for only 70, but by concerted effort it was somehow done.

The waiting ground crews and tower operators saw clusters of airplanes, flying in all directions with their landing lights on, skimming the frost covered tree tops, searching for the fog shrouded runways, the ground crews praying as they did their best to guide them in to a landing space. The men remember icicles hanging from the trees like stalactites, the big Fortresses looking like frosted chandeliers veiled in the fog and the coloured flares causing a rainbow effect.

There were many battle-scarred aircraft that night among those that returned almost out of fuel, groping for runways. A 92nd Bomb Group plane trying to find its way crash landed and burst into flames.

Many Canadians were put up for the night after their diverted aircraft landed. This was Christmas Eve. The 94th shared its Christmas dinner in keeping with the spirit of the season. Extra beds were provided for the 'guests' anywhere there was space, even tables with a blanket. For Christmas dinner, when the turkey ran short it was the hosts who got spam!

Later the 94th received many letters of thanks, citing them for the fine job they had done under such difficulties as hosts at Christmas.

The ground crews, who had worked all night in preparation for the next day's mission, staggered back to their huts and learned that the day's mission had been cancelled. Everyone was tired and weary. Morale flagged, but it really plummeted when it was learned of the death of Colonel Castle who had only recently been promoted to General and had been killed in action on Christmas Eve. He was a former commander of the 94th, beloved and respected by all members of the 94th. He left a true legend of leadership and respect in all the men of all ranks on the base. A quiet and respectful sorrow was evidenced all day on learning the sad news. Thus ended Christmas 1944 for the Americans. ■

Lalli Coppinger

Freezing fogs and wet snows have crystalized to cover this US 8th Air Force base at Bassingbourn with a shroud of white. Winter 1944-1945 was the severest in England in almost a generation. Prior to take-off, this 91st Bomb Group tail gunner clears the plexi-glass window in front of his gun sights.

·K·WHITLOCK·

Looking Back at World War II

An airman worships at an altar in Quidenham Parish Church, where the 96th Bomb Group, based at nearby Snetterton Heath, funded a stained glass memorial window.

It is Christmas 1944 and I am in the land of Dickens - real inns before me, real beefsteak, real ale drawn in pewter, open fireplaces, huge old oaken beams in the smoke-seasoned rooms filled with warmth and good cheer even though the country is in its fifth year of war.

I am stationed in a small Suffolk village that could have come right out of the pages of Dickens or off the front of a Christmas card. My bomber group of B-17s with the Eighth Air Force is stationed just northeast of London where we are engaged in flying long-range bombing missions to major cities in Germany. I am a teenage aerial gunner who has flown bombing runs through flak, clouded, fighter-infested, dangerous skies over Hitler's Festung Europa (Fortress Europe).

The oldest crewman in our team is 20 years old, the youngest 17 - none of us is eligible to vote.

Now it is Christmas Eve and I am going to St Mary's Church. I haven't been to church since being in England, but tonight, my third Christmas away from home, I feel I must be there. St Mary's is over 500 years old - unheated except for coal stoves and unlighted except for hundreds of candles burning around the inside of the church and on the altar. There is a deep snow on the ground and it is lighted by the gleaming candlelight shining through the frosted, stained glass.

As I enter the church I notice that it is filled with soldiers and civilians - except for one seat near the front. I make my way to this place and there is a music folio lying on the seat. I pick it up and hold it. The soldier in the next chair looks questioningly at me. During one part of the service the choir is to sing a special anthem. I did not know this. As we are all in uniform it is hard to distinguish which was the choir. I had taken the seat of a choir member who had not shown up for the service.

At the appointed time for the choir to sing, the soldier next to me nudges me and I stand up when they do. We sing beautifully, Silent Night, Holy Night, in that ancient place of worship. Then quietly file out into the winter night, back to our drab, cold barracks, but with a warm glow of a beautiful Christmas celebration in our hearts. It is a memorable one for me. I had never sung with a choir before ... and could not read music.

The next day our crew was shot down over Nuremberg, Germany and imprisoned for the duration of the war, but I had the special memory of that blessed night to carry me through the trials to come. ∎

Walter (Boots) Mayberry, Arizona

It was our first 48 hour pass from Rougham. Roy and I decided to hitch a ride into London. We hadn't heard about any big raids going on lately and we were looking forward to a good time in the big town!

We caught a ride on a lorry and saw the country from our perch on the top of a stack of lumber. After a long ride the driver pulled over somewhere and said "I'm turning right here, London's that way", pointing a finger ahead, "it's not far, you're on the outskirts, you can probably get another ride into the bright lights of London". He laughed when he said it because everyone knew that London, like everywhere else, was in total blackout. He dropped us off outside a pub. I forget what it was called - somebody's arms I think. I remember thinking that arms and heads were Britain's favourite parts of the anatomy when it came to naming pubs.

shrapnel. That stuff can kill ya." Over a friendly drink the Englishman told us how lethal the shrapnel was and especially right there, as there happened to be an anti-aircraft emplacement right at the rear of the pub.

After an hour or so, after it had quietened down outside, we left the warm and friendly atmosphere of the pub and ventured onto the streets which we found literally littered with razor sharp jagged pieces of shell fragments. We had learned our first British lesson in safety first. However, we almost goofed again before the weekend was over.

It was quite a busy one from the air raids point of view. In one neighbourhood a bomb had demolished a house in the middle of a residential row. There were people buried under the rubble, someone in the crowd told us. The building was still smoking when we ran

We thanked him and went inside for a quick drink only, as we were anxious to get to the real London where the action was. We were in the middle of sampling some of Britain's best warm beers when suddenly all hell seemed to break loose. We heard the wail of sirens and soon the pub vibrated with the impact and explosive sounds of the anti-aircraft fire. Reacting to our adrenolin we both rushed outside the pub and looked up at the blue-black sky. It was brilliant with searchlights. The noise of the ack-ack was deafening. Almost immediately we felt a strong grip on our shoulders as we were dragged forcibly back into the pub. It was our bartender. "What the hell d'you think you're doin? you wanna get killed?" he admonished us. "If ya wanna win this war you young fellas had better stay away from that

onto the street. The danger area was cordoned off and the rescue teams were assembled close to the building.

Without thinking, and disregarding the ropes, we eager beavers jumped over them, ready to help. We meant well, but were immediately stopped by the British Military and the National Fire Service, who shouted at us "Get out of here. That's an order. Leave this job to us - we know what we're doing". We did get the hell out of there, pronto, and had learned lesson no. 2, that it was better to leave certain jobs to those who had been trained for them. Our well meaning interference could easily have obstructed the work of qualified experts, and caused more havoc than help. ∎

Doyle Coppinger

Britain on the receiving end of aerial bombardment. Workmen clear the debris of demolished terraced houses in a Norfolk town.

Making Friends

Boys being taught the mysteries of baseball, 'a sort of rounders' to them.

A considerable number of friendships established between the Americans and the British during the war were to endure for a lifetime. A particular effort was made to encourage English families to offer the hospitality of their homes at Christmas when it was felt the GI would feel separation from 'his folks' the most. Sol Kupferman, serving with the 306th Bomb Group at Thurleigh, was involved in one of the successes:

"At Christmas 1943, British people near our base invited individual GIs to go along to their homes for the day. A Donald Nicoll went all out and accepted two of us (myself and Kenny Norris, a member of my crew) to share the holiday with his family. Don and his wife Dorothy were in their forties and they had a little six-year old daughter Cynthia. We knew all about how the English folks were rationed and about the shortages so we were prepared to go easy on eating and drinking. They couldn't have done more to make us feel at home. I took along a box of chocolates which was obviously a special treat. They made it last for several days; rationing themselves to one each per day. I don't think 'Cindy' had ever seen chocolates before. After dinner I played

They couldn't have done more to make us feel at home.

darts with the father, who was a prison guard. On that first visit I remember the Morrison table shelter in the dining room and the threadbare towels which they couldn't replace because of the rationing. This was the start of a lifetime friendship and during the rest of my time in England I accepted the Nicolls' invitation to use their spare bedroom whenever I had passes. The home life atmosphere they provided I feel sure helped me to survive. I recall making one mistake and that took place on 4th July, 1944. I went out into their backyard and shot off my .45 pistol into the air to celebrate. That sure upset Don Nicoll because he was the neighbourhood warden!"

It was not just the deprivations of wartime that the visitors were seeing. The low wages and salaries were reflected in the poorer domestic standards than would have been found in the homes of Americans with equivalent jobs. GIs were usually observant enough to be aware they were in low income homes and responded by taking presents, usually foodstuffs, that would be very welcome.

One section of the British community that the GI had no difficulty in making friends with

was the children. The bond was not just material as one might think from the legendary cry of "got any gum chum?" Whereas a British young man who considered himself adult distanced himself from juniors to affirm his recently attained status, the American placed no such barrier. There was no stigma in associating with youngsters or taking a condescending attitude towards them. British tongue-in-cheek sarcasm held that the popularity of children with Americans was not surprising as the latter had never really grown up. Yet what was done for their children in wartime was really appreciated.

Children's parties were periodically held on most USAAF bases where the hosts enjoyed themselves as much as their young guests. Undoubtedly the candy (sweets), chewing gum, chocolate bars, ice cream, oranges and other rare or unobtainable items that delighted young palates were a major attraction, but children also sensed they were not being patronised. Admittedly, these parties were encouraged by the US authorities who saw them as good public relations exercises. A War Orphans Fund was set up under the auspices of the US servicemen's newspaper, Stars and Stripes. The object being to provide additional financial aid for British children who had lost one or both parents from war action.

Many English boys were attracted to aircraft and in loitering around airfield boundaries were befriended by ground crewmen. Some youngsters even became mascots, fitted out with items of GI clothing. Others would willingly fetch and carry for their soldier friends. One lad at Mendlesham airfield had a regular out-of-school task of sweeping out the interior of his mechanic friend's bomber when it returned from operations. ■

1943 was the year that 'Father Christmas' arrived at Rougham, Bury St Edmunds with a big sackful of toys and goodies for a group of war orphans from Dr Barnardo's National Childrens' Homes.

Christmas with the 94th

Barnardo children would have had a much poorer Christmas had it not been for the big hearts of the Eighth Air Force men. The members of the 94th welcomed 145 children. They were provided with a bountiful dinner and greeted personally by Colonel Castle. The men of the 94th had been saving gum, candy and cookie rations for this occasion. They had also collected and contributed money to finance the party and all the necessary adornments. While in London, on pass, they had been buying toys which they secretly tested for proper performance and to satisfy the whims of each age

After the entertainment Father Christmas called the name of each child, who received a gift from under the brilliantly lit tree. In each child's surprise package was a radio. Colonel Castle then presented to each of the Homes assorted games and athletic equipment. The base band played God Save the King and the Star Spangled Banner.

Some 50 men from every section of the base had served on special committees and helped in the programme. It was a total effort that came right from the heart.

Christmas party at Molesworth for the local English kids. All the airmen at the base subscribed to the presents handed out to each young guest.

group. Maybe all of them reverted to childhood for a time. The men had requested Christmas decorations from home and received good response. Committees were formed.

Christmas carols were played by the base band. Folk tunes and trick fiddling by a corporal from Kentucky and a wonderful rendition of White Christmas by Cpl Planisek of Cleveland, who the night before had been peeling potatoes. The Ordnance Section Chief awed the children with a flashy rendition on his accordian, which was followed by tap dancing. Then the children's choir and morris dancers entertained the men. There were skits and cartoons and finally Father Christmas. These Americans had talent, but more than that they had big hearts. It was hard to say who had the most fun, the kids or the Yanks!

Maybe there are Barnardo children, now grown, who were among those who attended that 1943 Christmas party at Rougham, who still remember the good time they had and the Yanks who gave it to them. ∎

Lalli Coppinger

The Romances

The Second World War had a profound effect on a large proportion of young British women who volunteered for the Services and essential war work, or were conscripted. It gave them a new-found freedom and liberation from parental influence and the usual pattern of female conformity.

The uncertainty of life in the war years added to this release. The coming of the GI added yet another dimension; these young men's brashness made them exciting, part of the Hollywood image come true. This could later have led to disillusion but these girls found that once one got to know these young men, most were kind, courteous and fun. Additionally, by most accounts, they were more romantically inclined than British boys. They certainly had something special for an estimated 70,000 British women who married American servicemen.

Dances were the frequent starting point for relationships but perhaps as many that resulted in permanence came about in a variety of ways, so often characterised by the young man's persistence after a first sighting, a normal entry into courtship the world over.

The obvious place to make contact with girls was dance halls and the GIs found plenty in the UK. Apart from the regular every night dance halls in big towns and cities, dances were a regular feature of smaller public halls - and many village halls had one every Saturday night.

In all the GIs soon began to influence behaviour. Foxtrot and waltzes were reduced to a close in shuffle with ones partner which ballroom dancing enthusiasts criticised as being an excuse for a mobile embrace. Quicksteps brought the jitterbugging exponents onto the floor and many a girl discovered that 'let's cut a rug honey' was not an invitation to get to work on a carpet with a pair of scissors. There were some aspects of the British dance hall scene that were strange to GIs as Al Zimmerman of the 493rd Bomb Group found:

Doyle and Lalli Coppinger at their wedding in London, October 1944. The bride's parents are also present.

"The place to go in London to dance was the converted opera house near Covent Garden. It was here that I first took the floor with a British gal. All was going fine until another girl tried to cut in, grabbed me by the arm and tried to pull me away. I'd been told the English girls were shy and reserved and here's one trying to pull me away from another! Embarrassed, I just held on to the girl I had, said "How do you do" and kept dancing. My partner's immediate reaction was offence. What was I doing not taking the other girl? I was bewildered until it was explained that this was a ladies' 'Excuse Me' dance. When a girl tapped your shoulder you changed partners". ■

We were on a bomb run, 24 September 1944 and I was discharging 'Chaff', the metallic foil strips that jammed radar beams. At the time I was pretty scared, I could hear the thump of flak bursting all around. When I opened one chaff box I found a slip of paper with a handwritten note. It read:

"If you've no girl friend to care where you roam

And if you've no wife sitting waiting at home

If you'd care for a pen friend, then now is the time

To sit down and write Joy or Winnie a line.

This was such a surprise I forgot all about the flak while looking at this note and wondering what the girls were like.

Back at base I sent them a letter which must have been heavily censored because their reply indicated they thought I was writing from Italy. We were never able to arrange a meeting but I still have the note and the memory of the time two English girls made the air war momentarily stop for me high in the sky over Germany.

Daniel Freitas

Approval for an Anglo-American marriage was by no means easy, particularly in the girl's case.

Most parents were not eager to see a daughter entwined with a man from a faraway land, of whose background they knew little and of whom what they had been told could rarely be confirmed. This protectiveness was strong enough in some cases to prevent the union and in others it took time before parents came to terms with the prospect. Cecilia Trip, the English half of a happy marriage had her father making the initial move:

"Daddy met him somewhere and invited him to call, but failed to advise Mummy of the fact. One evening this Yank comes knocking on our front door wanting to know if Mr Smith was home. No, but we expected Daddy shortly if he would care to come in and wait. He did, and showed up the following eight evenings. It was quickly obvious that Daddy wasn't the attraction. The relationship developed steadily but when we decided to marry Daddy wasn't very happy. I was the only child and he didn't like the thought of me going to America which seemed so remote from England in those days of long sea journeys. But Daddy had no one to blame but himself; he was the one who had invited the Yank home!"

No doubt many American mothers were apprehensive on hearing their sons had taken a British bride but the principal caution, which almost amounted to opposition in the early days, was expressed by the US authorities. This manifested itself at unit level with the prospective bridegroom being interviewed by the CO or his delegate and the base chaplain of the man's denomination. The pitfalls of such a proposed alliance were pointed out and the soldier asked to think again. The girl also had to have an interview with the base chaplain and, if she were of another religious denomination to her intended husband, this could be particularly hard. When the trickle of marriages became a flood these interviews mellowed considerably. Robert Cayer was faced with the official attitude that existed in 1942:

"I was one of the first men at Bassingbourn to have an English bride. I didn't drink and was having tea and sandwiches at some function in a church hall and got talking to a girl in British Army uniform, the ATS. When I asked for a date she backed off and said that I'd better write her a letter to ask! Never met such a shy girl. Well, eventually she accepted my proposal of marriage but the chaplain was told to try and talk me out of it. Don't think the US Army was too keen on its men marrying foreign girls at that time. To complicate matters I was Catholic and my future wife Protestant. In the end the chaplain was convinced that I knew what I was doing and said go ahead.

GIs who married usually only had contact with wives when on leave. Those members of ground personnel on 'permanent' stations were more fortunate and when not on duty were permitted to live off base. Marion Smith of the 4th Strategic Air Depot was one:

"Got married in October 1944 and we had a room in my wife's sister's house in Sproughton Road, Ipswich. Providing I was in by 7 o'clock in the morning I was allowed to spend the night off base. It was about 10 miles from the Hitcham depot and for the rest of my time in England I cycled there after coming off duty and back each morning. The trip took about an hour and in the cold and the blackout it wasn't easy". ■

"Will you take this woman ....."
S/Sgt Henry Corley and his bride at their wedding in Quidenham church, Norfolk. The service is being conducted by Captain Charles Smith.

Without doubt the most famous British institution as far as the GI was concerned was the pub, for there was nothing that truly corresponded to this in the USA.

Sgts Robinson and Bennett out for an evening visit to a Suffolk pub.

On arrival in the UK, servicemen were advised by the military authorities that the public house or inn was as much for social intercourse as for drinking and that most pubs had their 'regulars' who met to enjoy the company of friends 'over a pint'. Pubs were a natural starting point for any Yank who wanted to meet Limeys and to learn about the people and the country. There were a lot of pubs, particularly in East Anglia where towns like Ipswich, Bury St Edmunds and Norwich seemed to have at least one pub in every street. Much like the natives, individual GIs settled on one or two particular pubs, usually after learning that there were those that only catered for working class trade, some for the well-to-do (although they usually advertised themselves as hotels), while most catered for class and pocket by a public bar and a saloon, the latter having higher charges for purchases. There were also additional rooms in many houses with such curious names as Snug, Tap Room, Pot Room and others.

For those unbriefed, British beer was often a disappointment as it was not the lager type beer popular in the States. In the first place it was rather flat and, secondly, it was not chilled. Cold drinks were available in certain hotels in big cities but a refrigerator was a rare facility in the average pub. There was some variety: pale ale, bitter, brown stout and special beers such as Bass and Guinness, but all quite different from the beer in the bars back home. The GIs regularly complained about the warm, flat beer but many soon developed a taste for it. The alcohol strength was variable. Even so, as many an unwary drinker discovered, it could have quite a kick. Getting drunk was no problem. Roger Armstrong, a radio operator in the 91st Bomb Group at Bassingbourn, recalls "We were admonished to be temperate in our consump-

Pubs were a natural starting point for any Yank who wanted to meet Limeys and to learn about the people and the country.

tion of English beer. We were reminded that American beer was 3.2 per cent alcohol whereas the British beer was strong enough to make our tongues 'wag at both ends'. Since I was not much of a drinker the warm beer did

The GIs regularly complained about the warm, flat beer but many soon developed a taste for it.

not bother me. In fact, I acquired a taste for it." Earl Robinson, an armourer with the 479th Fighter Group at Wattisham, also found the beer strange and warm, but what really surprised him was when he saw some old men in a pub stick a poker in the fire and, when red hot, stick it in their pint of beer to make it even warmer!

The supply of beer was limited by the brewer who rationed each public house to a specified amount every week. The ration would have catered for the requirements of the regulars without reduction of their consumption. With Allied servicemen stationed in the vicinity of the pub, the ration did not endure for long. Some publicans endeavoured to restrict customers on a daily basis; most simply sold on demand and then put out 'No Beer' signs until the next supply. It became a habit for some GIs to drain a pub and then move elsewhere, a tactic that made them very unpopular with the regulars. Particularly when the regulars were working late. At a Dedham farm the harvesters were always treated to a pint in the local pub after a day's work. One evening in August 1944 the harvesters arrived for their well deserved sustenance to be met outside by Willie Frost, one of their band who had gone ahead of the rest. "Wha's the matter, Willie?" His anger was

Autographs still to be seen on the wall inside The Swan at Lavenham. (Photograph by Gillian Oke, The Image Factory.)

plain to see. "No beer" he hissed. "No beer? That were only due in this afternoon. What's happened?" another harvester queried. "Why, the bloody Yanks of course. They've bin here early and drunk the place dry." Willie lived to be 80 but he never had a good word for Uncle Sam after that evening. A countryman will forgive most misdemeanours, but he who deprives him of his beer is an enemy for life.

Another irritation was the deeper pocket of the GI who could afford liberal amounts of ale. By 1944 a pint of bitter was 15 pence (25 cents) which was expensive for a farm worker whose standard wage was the equivalent of 50 pints. However, the average GI was generous and regularly treated those acquaintances in his adopted pub. Hard liquor was more difficult to find and what few bottles a publican could acquire were kept 'under the counter' for favoured customers. Many Americans were in this category although at 25 shillings a bottle (5 dollars) it was expensive even to them.

The pub was a place for talking and also introduced the GI to the table games of Shove Ha'penny and Cribbage as well as the dartboard on the wall. Lt Robert Coffin was introduced to darts during off-duty visits: "I soon found I was pretty good at it. Guess it didn't go down too well with the old English guys in the Three Cocks at Brigstock as they tried to make out that when I threw a dart it might go anywhere. As soon as I walked in the pub door they would shout. "Grab your tin hat and take cover, that Yank's here.""

Another feature of the pub was musical entertainment, singing round a piano, and GIs would often join in. WAC Eleanor Frederick's observation was that in pubs you often saw a British boy sit down and play the piano, as most pubs had one in the saloon. At that time it would have been most unusual to see an American serviceman do this as he would have been looked upon as being a cissy.

Many country pubs and those in the poorer town districts were very basic establishments, while those at the other end of the market provided considerable comfort and good amenities. Lt Jack Bryant recalls how very basic was the first pub he visited near his Sudbury base. "After partaking of various beverages over the course of the evening it was necessary to make use of a facility euphemistically called a 'water closet'. A closet it certainly was not. It was outside at the back of the building and consisted of a partially enclosed slate wall with a diagonal trough at the base. There was no lighting because of the blackout requirements and overcast clouds limited any natural light. It was not quite pitch black, but it was close to it.

A countryman will forgive most misdemeanours, but he who deprives him of his beer is an enemy for life.

Two or three local customers were occupying the available space, facing the wall, while I waited my turn. Then one of the Englishmen spoke to another beside him, showing a forbearance impossible for an American. What he said was "Pardon me old chap but you're urinating on my leg"".

The GI took readily to the wartime pastime of autographing walls and ceilings. Where they were allowed, British servicemen left their signature on pubs they had visited, a practice which spread to their ally, but was very much dependent on the goodwill of the landlord. Most of this graffiti was removed in post-war years as being unsightly. In a few places it was seen in a different light and has been preserved, notably at The Swan, Lavenham and The Eagle in Cambridge. Some famous names are among those left by American customers during the war years. ∎

A Party to Remember

We had just flown the north Atlantic route via Greenland and Iceland to Prestwick, Scotland. We got as far as Cheddington in the English midlands, it was our first stop- over in the UK. This was near a small rural market town called Dunstable, as yet not too familiar with Americans, much less airmen.

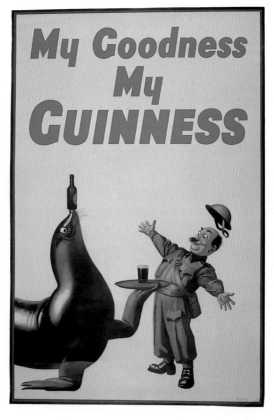

A 1940s advertisement for Guinness. (Reproduced by kind permission of Guinness Brewing GB, London.)

The first place we went was a pub in the middle of the town. A group of us crowded up to the bar. We had been there only a short time when somebody in the group suggested that we make a party and asked the bar keeper if she could tell us what the entire stock of liquor and beer in the pub was worth. Quite taken aback by this request the bar keeper went behind the bar and into the back office to talk to the owner. She came back in a matter of minutes with the owner in tow. The owner was as much surprised as she was and asked us why we had made this request. We said we had just that day arrived in merry old England and were heading for combat duty. We wanted to have a party and in order to do so we needed a goodly supply of hard spirits. The pub owner got out his pencil and paper and figured out how much the liquor in the pub was worth. He handed the

piece of paper to one of the officers who looked at it and immediately dug into his pockets and took off his hat and passed it round to the others in our group.

"That'll do it lads" said the pub owner as he counted out the money on the bar, adding that the place was theirs for the party. For the rest of that evening we had one huge party staying in the pub until closing time. I recall running to catch the tailboard of the last convoy truck out of town back to the base and just managed to grab it in the darkness of the blackout. We left the next day for our combat base at Shipdham and never saw that town or pub again but I will always remember that party. ∎

Forrest S Clark

Sharing a few pints with the locals. Mostly middle aged and pensioners; the young men were in the British service. Many GI's met and made friends in pubs.

Officially or otherwise, GIs were at liberty to make bicycle explorations of the surrounding countryside in the evenings. With a pass the evening Liberty Run to the local town or city would be taken. It was often a Liberty Run convoy of a half dozen 6" x 6" trucks or British ex-civilian buses, with a 1900 hours departure and 2300 hours return.

Miss Adelaide Johnson, from New York City, one of the first American Red Cross nurses to arrive in London, photographed on her first visit to the Milestone Club, Kensington.

Red Cross Clubs

Apart from the pubs and cinemas, and on some nights dance halls, some large towns had a Red Cross Club. These were set up and administered by the American Red Cross organisation using a requisitioned hotel or large house. Amenities included a cafeteria, games room, lounges where the latest periodicals could be read and with letter writing facilities. The scope, of course, depended on the space available and the size of the venue but all were well patronised by the local USAAF community. There were also Anglo-American Clubs sponsored by the Anglo-American Hospitality Committees of local people to promote and foster goodwill. The amenities were not so extensive as in the Red Cross Clubs, but they were excellent places for gaining introductions to British families.

Leave periods depended on the discretion and requirements of unit commanders; enlisted men ('other ranks' to the British) usually being able to obtain a 48 hour pass once a month. Officers had more flexible arrangements while combat crew airmen were often allowed two or three day passes during periods when the unit was 'stood down'. The favourite destination was London and there were few long-stay GIs that did not visit the capital city. Apart from the historic and entertainment attractions, there were, eventually 15 Red Cross Clubs in central London alone. Seven were strictly for enlisted men, four for officers and one, at 10 Charles Street, purely for women officers. The others catered for both officers and men, the most famous and largest being Rainbow Corner in Shaftesbury Avenue. Rainbow Corner, opened in December 1942, could host 2,000 men at a time and had a staff of over 400, the majority British, with American Red Cross employees holding administrative positions. This was also the usual form of staffing at the Red Cross Clubs in metropolitan areas. Large military bases also had American Red Cross facilities. Every major airfield had an Aero Club staffed by three American Red Cross girls with some help from local women.

Many of those who worked at Red Cross Clubs were volunteers, in London several being women of some prominence. For Al Zimmerman of the 493rd Bomb Group, the dominant feature of his first visit to Rainbow Corner was one such personality:

"At Rainbow Corner there was this lovely lady in an American Red Cross uniform who sat at a desk in one of the rooms. A sign on the desk read "Have Adèle Astair write a letter home for you". Adèle Astair was the sister of Fred Astair, the famous movie tap-dancer. She was also Lady Cavendish, having married into British nobility. I was one of the fascinated guys who went over to ask her to write a letter home for me, but I really did it so I could stare at her; I think she had the most gorgeous set of legs I've ever seen in my life." ■

Some US nurses seen arriving at the American Red Cross Milestone Club in London, and some of the GIs who were ready to give them a warm welcome.

Many hotels in London's West end were turned into American Red Cross Clubs in WWII, after the arrival of the Americans. The Washington Hotel in London's Mayfair district was for enlisted men and one of the busiest, second only to the famed Rainbow Corner at Shaftesbury Avenue.

The Washington Club was smaller, cosier, more intimate than Rainbow Corner, where home-sick Yanks could sit on a couch in a fairly quiet lobby and write letters home, get a room for about the equivalent of two dollars, eat in the cafeteria, dance up a storm to a good band and maybe meet a nice girl who wouldn't steal their wallet. The girls were screened. I was one of them for about two years.

As a volunteer hostess I learned a lot about the young American male, far from home, 1940s type. They weren't the kind that we English girls had become familiar with through American movies. Sure, they were from big cities, some were sophisticated, but they were also from every small town and hamlet in the USA. Their average age was 19-23. I met a few who were even younger than 19 - they'd lied about their age. And there were many who had never tasted hard liquor or smoked, and had little or no adult sexual experience. At the most vulnerable time of their lives, with adrenolin pumping, raging hormones and all, they were let loose in London, at that period the largest city in the world, with just about every temptation known to man available to them. London was renowned for its wide variety of entertainment as many an unsuspecting GI found out, not always to his advantage. But they learned fast and these were the men who frequented the Red Cross Clubs, the 'safe havens' from the blackout! ■

Lalli Coppinger

Collecting Thetford girls for the Saturday night dance.

I started to go to dances when I was 16 years old and one Saturday night I went with some friends to the Oddfellows Hall at Weldon ...

The music was Glenn Miller, who was playing live over the radio. There were large windows in the hall with big sills on which we girls put our handbags. While I was dancing, a group of Americans came in and sat on the chairs below the window where we girls had been sitting. When I went to get my handbag I said "Excuse me, can I get my bag?". And this Yank says "I'll think about it". Cheeky so-and-so. Anyway, he asked me to dance to 'In the Mood' and later he wanted to take me home. Now we girls had heard lots of things about these Yanks and were not sure what we might be getting ourselves into. So if you let one you weren't sure about take you home, then the thing was to take him to the wrong house so he didn't know where you lived. My mother had no time for Americans but a few nights later she came in and said "There's a Yank walking up and down the road outside with a torch, asking for you." As she

was worried what the neighbours would think she told me to go out and ask him in. It was the same fellow and it was the start of our courtship.

One night I lent him my brand new bicycle to go back to the base. The next I heard he'd got burned in an explosion and was detained in Lilford hospital. While he was there I borrowed a bike and cycled the 30 miles round trip to see him. When he came out he found my new bike had been stolen, but he promised that one day he'd buy me another one. We married in the summer of 1944 when I was 17 and went to London for our honeymoon. It took Bob a long while to keep his promise, but eventually, after eight grandchildren, he did buy me a new bike.

Stella Auger

One night we had a dance at our 9th Air Force base. At the intermission the GI band marched up and down the floor which had been decorated like a football field since it was in the fall. The band started playing college football songs which were completely unknown to the British girls, but greatly stirred up the Americans. It turned the crowd into a frenzy and someone came up with a football and soon the roughest game in history was in progress on the dance floor. Finally the colonel called a halt saying "Some of you guys have to fly tomorrow". I walked back to a very stunned lady who asked "What was all that about?" Realizing that she couldn't possibly understand about college songs I said "For a few minutes we were back home at the best time of the year - the football season". She pondered this a couple of seconds and retorted "Well I hope you Yanks don't act that way all the time when you're home".

Jack Sloan, California

Womens Land Army girls from the Culford Hostel in Suffolk enjoy an evenings dancing with GIs. The girls' uniforms did nothing for a feminine appearance, but a sizeable number of land army girls married US servicemen.

Music

One of the greatest pleasures brought to East Anglia by the Americans was their music.

One of the best remembered of the dance bands is the one formed from scratch by a group of young musicians, both officers and enlisted men, attached to the 94th Bomb Group. To form an orchestra under normal circumstances is not easy, but for men stationed on a rural airbase, in a foreign country, in the middle of a world war, it would seem to be highly improbable, if not altogether impossible to achieve. But the Skymasters did it!

They had help and encouragement from their superiors and Special Services but their own team work and enthusiasm provided the greatest incentive for them to become a very popular band in their part of East Anglia, which finally culminated in them making a recording at the RCA Victor Studios in London on 12th June 1945. At first, some of the instruments left much to be desired, and according to one band member, they were fixed up with all manner of odds and ends, including chewing gum and an item of rubber goods intended for a different purpose! Their practice sessions could never be relied upon because of changes in duties, missions etc. The war came first and they learned to be flexible. They were always scouting around for different musicians. At one time they couldn't locate any brass, but managed a couple of violinists. Because there was a tendency to transfer to other duties the players changed from time to time. A member states that many of the trumpet men were gunners, and were hard to come by. The bass player describes his bass fiddle as an old five stringer which projected the sound in front, while he stood behind it, so he had a hard time hearing what he was playing. He plucked the strings so hard he said, mostly in the 4-beat mode, that his fingers "had blisters on top of blisters".

The Skymasters Dance Band, 1944.

As the band improved and spread out farther afield the members had the worry of getting back to the base in one piece, often at breakneck speed on a GI truck through the inky blackness of the English country lanes. One crew chief from Montana said that he was always dreading the prospect that he might oversleep his preflight wakeup. He bunked next to where other crews were working all night on engine problems. He says he lost a lot of sleep waking up too early with the noise, thinking he'd overslept, and after rushing half asleep outside, he found himself out there all alone.

The band had two leaders, the first one from its inception early in 1943, and subsequently another, a trumpet player who was also an arranger, and whose professional know-how gave the band its more perfected 'polish'.

The Skymasters played at Red Cross Clubs, civilian dances and base parties. During December 1944 alone, they performed 27 nights out of 31. They didn't even have time for rehearsals, but 'just read the stuff on the job'. ∎

Lalli Coppinger

The Rockets play for the 381st Bomb Group enlisted men's dance at the Aero Club on 6 July 1944.

The Glenn Miller USAAF Band was organized at Yale University, New Haven, CT, in 1943. For nearly a year, enlarged to 45 members (with a complete string section), the band presented Saturday broadcasts on NBC radio ... concerts called 'I Sustain the Wings'. At Miller's insistence, the band was moved to England in June 1944.

Major Glenn Miller's loss on December 15th 1944, came as a complete and devastating surprise to the whole world.

Miller, along with Flight Officer John RS Morgan (pilot) and Lt Col Norman P Baessell (8th AF Service Command), left Twinwood Farm airfield (near Bedford) in a single-engined Noorduyn Norseman (No. 70285) for Paris, disappeared and was never heard from again.

Three days later, when the cross-channel weather improved, Lt Don Haynes, the band administrative officer, and the entire band flew to Paris, to find the Norseman and its passengers had never arrived. Haynes wrote of this later:

"There's been no trace of Glenn, the passenger or the pilot, since that foggy Friday afternoon when I alone saw them off. Glenn took the trip that I was to make. He decided to go in my place. I brought the outfit over three days later only to find that Glenn had not arrived. Our trip was uneventful ... but not his."

Since that fatal day, many stories of what had happened have surfaced, the search for facts and proof still goes on, and the Miller disappearance has grown to legendary proportion, numerous tales yet to be proven. One such

The Glenn Miller Enigma

A programme from one of the band's concerts signed by Major Glenn Miller.

tale believed by many researchers to be the most plausible, is told by the pilot and navigator of an RAF Lancaster bomber. They had taken off at noon on December 15th 1944, to bomb railway yards at Siegen, Germany, but their mission was aborted due to bad weather. The pilot, Victory Gregory, and navigator, Fred Shaw, told of the bomber mission being aborted because of bad weather. They were instructed to jettison their bombs over the English Channel and they reported seeing the bombs explode far below and a small aircraft (said to be a Norseman) fall into the sea, "presumably crippled by the shock waves."

Alan Ross of Liverpool, England, a member of a long-standing Glenn Miller Appreciation Society, investigated the claim. The English Defense Ministry checked records and reported that December 15th was a foggy day, "not even the pigeons were flying," that the Lancasters took off at noon and were returning from the aborted flight at about the same time the Miller aircraft would have been over the Channel. Reportedly, the Norseman left the air base near Bedford (50 miles north of London) at 1:55 pm, without a flight plan and 'course unknown'.

Robert E Wilson

The above is just one of the many stories about the probable theories on Glenn Miller's disappearance.

Glenn Miller's superb 'AEF band', as the American Band of the Allied Expeditionary Forces was conveniently termed, was in Britain for six months (28th June to 18th December 1944). Although primarily in the UK to entertain the huge numbers of American servicemen in the European Theatre of Operations, the band was extremely popular with millions of Britons. They knew it through radio broadcasts.

The band (two officers and 62 enlisted men, 40 of them musicians) was based at Bedford until it went to the Continent in December. It made changes at Co-Partners Hall, which had been a gas company's social club, and the little place was used exclusively by the AEF band for rehearsals and broadcasts. As with other buildings in the town used by the BBC, it was connected with Broadcasting House by landline, so that broadcasts could be made. Recordings were also fed to Broadcasting House. Bedford Corn Exchange was also used by the band for broadcasts and concerts, playing in the main hall.

On the wall of Bedford Corn Exchange is a large metal plaque dedicated by the Glenn Miller Society "to the everlasting memory of Major Alton Glenn Miller, 1904 'The Moonlight Serenader'; 1944, Director of the American Band of the Allied Expeditionary Forces, for his outstanding contribution to popular music, recalling his concerts to the Allied forces at this hall during 1944. This commemorative plaque was unveiled at a tribute concert by the Million Airs Orchestra at the Corn Exchange, Bedford, on February 28, 1976."

The Corn Exchange, as well as being used for concerts and broadcasts, housed a Forces

Major Glenn Miller, at Attlebridge airfield, with John Woolnough who founded the 8th Air Force Historical Society.

canteen. The town was a centre for many British Army and RAF personnel and, after the USA entered the war, the Americans, too, as the Eighth Air Force moved into bases near Bedford.

Dances and concerts with music in the Miller style are still held in the Corn Exchange. ∎

The United States Army Air Forces band play an open air concert.

Remember the Yanks

During the war years they were often called 'the Bloody Yanks', for initially there was a general disapproval of the exuberant young men who began to appear in our towns and countryside. Not so much personal disapproval, but a reflection of the prevalent British attitude that the Yanks were all talk and hadn't much stomach for a fight; this itself having something to do with big prosperous cousin taking over the Allied direction of the war effort. As a 14 year old I was not immune from this unfair view and, with my school chums, was quick to dismiss the high airfields, arranged for my cousin and myself to inspect one of the USAAF A-20 Havoc light bombers based at Horham. This was a great thrill for we boys although we were somewhat astonished to find this particular aircraft filled with canned candies, cigarette cartons and toilet rolls! Our disdain was reflected in our speculation as to the need for the latter. What we did not know was that this aircraft was about to set off to operate from North Africa where the crew knew conditions would be primitive and that there would be few luxuries.

US military personnel have been in the UK for a half century but when the older generations of Britishers talk about the Yanks it is usually a reference to the Second World War presence.

claims of enemy aircraft shot down by the Fortress and Liberator aerial gunners as typical Yank exaggeration. Nevertheless, as an aeroplane mad youth I was soon to relish the American presence in the East Anglian sky.

Like many of my generation, before 1939 the most desired occupation when one 'grew up' was on the footplate of an express locomotive. Within a year the fascination for steam locomotives had been abandoned for the dream of being a fighter pilot. Young eyes were frequently turned skywards at the ever-mounting activity. Late in 1942 an RAF officer uncle, who had the task of opening up new

Silhouetted against the early morning sun, a Liberator is seen taking off from the runway, with a ground crewman waving in the foreground.

In June 1943 the airfield that had been carved out of farmland only a mile from my home was ready for occupation. We boys longed for RAF Spitfires. In the event sixty-four Martin B-26 Marauder medium bombers and two and a half thousand young Americans arrived. Their coming quickly provided a new dimension to our interest. Nearly all the aircraft had nicknames painted on their noses in addition to comic motifs or quite revealing nudes. Unbeknown to the aviators, several Marauders were 'adopted', their fortunes followed from vantage points on the neighbouring public road through regular appraisals of the symbols painted on nose sides - for combat missions flown and enemy fighters claimed shot down. My Marauder was called 'Privy Donna' and carried a motif featuring a winged 'outhouse' dispensing bombs. Its selection had nothing to do with the lavatorial leanings of a schoolboy but rather the proximity of the aircraft's parking place to a gap in the roadside hedge. At first the American MPs endeavoured to keep locals moving along the public road bordering the western side of the airfield. Curiosity brought people from nearby villages and towns to view the then novelty of locally based aircraft, although I fancy the large number of young girls in attendance were more interested in the men who flew and serviced the Marauders. No doubt appreciating it was a pointless exercise, the base authorities eventually withdrew the regular MP Jeep patrols that tried to keep people moving and spectators were no longer barred.

What was seen at the local airfield was soon to change our opinion of the Yanks. Perhaps summed up by the local butcher's son, once an ardent critic who, watching a combat mission return one evening pronounced: "No-one is going to tell me the Yanks can't fly and fight".

"No-one is going to tell me the Yanks can't fly and fight".

Certainly the activity on our doorstep brought home the grim reality of the air war, most notably the empty parking places when a bomber failed to return. There were specific incidents that left lasting impressions, none more so than a warm July day in 1943 when a badly shot-up Fortress staggered into the landing pattern. One could literally see daylight through holes in the wings and tailplane. The ambulances in attendance indicated casualties - seven wounded of the ten men on board was the rumour. Those BBC news reports of the bomber offensive over Hitler's empire were suddenly given substance. No-one disagreed with the butcher's son. The Marauders, Liberators and Fortresses had become just as much 'our' aircraft as the Halifaxes, Stirlings and Lancasters.

The Marauders at our airfield were eventually replaced by fighter squadrons with aircraft carrying even more flamboyant decor. There was the occasion when the youthful 'plane watchers' at the roadside were approached by a pilot. Lt Richard Heineman wanted to know if we would like to look at his Thunderbolt. An unbelievable invitation from a real fighter pilot! We were through the boundary hedge and barbed wire like greased lightning. Had we any sisters? My friend had three (old enough to be of interest) and immediately received most attention from our host. My friend was even allowed to sit in the cockpit! I only had a brother and would dearly have liked

Captain Frederick J Christensen, an ace from the 'Zemke Wolf Pack' - the top scoring US fighter group in England - holder of the Air Medal and three clusters, Distinguished Flying Cross, the four clusters and the Silver Star.

to arrange a sex change for him at that moment. A few days later Richard Heineman's colourful Thunderbolt was no longer to be seen at its usual place. We assumed it was in the hangar or had been relocated to another part of the base. Unbeknown to us in those war days, Richard Heineman had been shot down and killed in an air fight, probably an incident recorded as a victory symbol on some Luftwaffe pilot's Messerschmitt.

Having left school to meet the need for extra agricultural labour, my prime indulgence received a boost when my father was asked to farm fields taken over for the air base but left unused. Equipped with a pass, I could actually enter onto the flying field itself - ostensibly in pursuance of farming duties. Here the generosity of the GI was encountered: "Say kid, would you like some candy?" The sweets were welcome but the fact that they were given me by the head mechanic of fighter ace Fred Christensen's

Tea party with her folks. Two GIs socialise with an English family in Norfolk. Dad is smoking a gift cigar - no doubt brought from the PX (the servicemens' store).

Thunderbolt was the real accolade. Then there was the evening after haymaking near the perimeter track when through the hedge from the road a very large sergeant appeared. "Hey Pop", he addressed my father "any chance of a lift to the other side of the airfield?" My father said we were just leaving and invited the sergeant to enter our large Talbot saloon. He was, to say the least, surprised when the sergeant called back to the hole in the hedge from whence he had come: "Okay you guys, we ain't got to foot it back to camp after all." There appeared another GI, then another and another; they kept coming. "I don't think we are going to be able to squeeze you all in," my father said diplomatically. To no avail; the throng was already squeezing into the Talbot. The air was heavy with beery breath and it was evident that there were some very happy men present. The happiest was the large sergeant and I ended up riding on his lap. He held a yellow rose in his right hand, which he periodically jammed under my father's and my nose, with the joyous

The air was heavy with beery breath and it was evident that there were some very happy men present.

explanation: "The lady at The Fox gave me this real English rose out of her garden. Don't that smell just cute? A real English rose!" We agreed it did smell cute, although its fragrance was drowned by the overpowering beery atmosphere in the overloaded car. The old Talbot slowly but safely made the other side of the airfield, despite the rear tyres occasionally rubbing the mudguards. As they disembarked the GIs cascaded coins onto the rear seat despite my father's protestations that it was unnecessary. After the thirteen GIs - yes, thirteen - staggered away, I gathered up over £5, a

fortune to a boy earning 15 shillings a week. Unfortunately, my father decided it was far too large a sum for me and pocketed it himself.

The average Britisher did not appreciate the nature of the US populace. After an evening's harvesting or haymaking the farm workers would be treated to a pint at the local hostelry. Here shoulders were rubbed with GIs and conversations pursued. After one bout of refreshment, Willie, an Essex stalwart, emerged somewhat troubled. "That Yank I bin talking to. He's really a bloody Germin! His father and mother were Germins and he was born in Germiny!" The fact that the GI concerned was undoubtedly as true to the USA as its founding fathers would have been difficult for Willie and many like him to comprehend in those parochial days. On another occasion when imbibing at The Crown, a GI asked about our farming practices and said he was previously a cowboy. Detecting scepticism he took a cart rope from a tractor and trailer parked outside, twirled the rope above his head and lassoed old Horry, who was standing 30 feet away. Horry was not amused; we were all amazed.

There was no doubt about the attraction American servicemen had for a large proportion of local womanhood. Many girls had amorous

We got to know their genuine generosity; they gave and expected nothing in return.

liaisons with them (I plead guilty to being a witness in some cases) and several became GI brides, including a landgirl on our farm. A benefit which I derived from this match was copies of 'The Stars and Stripes', the US forces daily newspaper, which her husband passed on after he had read them. The feature which drew my attention (and also my father's) was the cartoon strips. The adventures of Li'l Abner, Dick Tracy and Terry and the Pirates being far more entertaining than anything that appeared in British publications. And in those days of shortages and clothes rationing other passdowns were a boon. For years I wore the lightweight GI shoes, which had rubber soles in contrast to our usual studded heavy leather and GI cotton caps which were washable. Fortunate were the locals who had a friendly GI benefactor. We got to know their genuine generosity; they gave and expected nothing in return. When our farm grass mower broke down on the airfield a sergeant from the nearby machine shop took it in and effected repairs in his free time.

By the summer of 1944 the Yanks had become an accepted part of life in East Anglia and the East Midlands. The sky rarely failed to hold one of their aircraft and hundreds were not uncommon. The throb of aero engines seemed incessant. The familiar 'OD' uniforms were rarely absent from our towns and villages where a Yank leaning against a wall watching the world go by, or pedalling his bike down the middle of the road, was a familiar sight. They were to leave a considerable impression on those who knew them, which did not easily fade when they departed. In the immediate post-war years a flock of home-going rooks might for an instant be mistaken for a formation of returning Fortresses; a tractor starting in a winter's dawn could momentarily be the life-burst of an unsilenced aero engine on the near-by airfield. But even now there are times when the far off burble of young voices raises the ghosts of North American laughter floating through the leafy English lanes as of long ago. ∎

Roger A Freeman

A group of English children who are guests at a 'kiddies party' given by the 379th Bomb Group, gather around a YB-40 Fortress.

Friends of the Eighth (FOTE)

FOTE is an informal organisation, formed in 1972, by a nucleus of individuals interested in preserving the history of the United States 8th Air Force.

From the interest generated, friendships have developed over the intervening years between the various 8th Air Force veterans' associations in America and FOTE members. Memorials to those who never returned have been erected at former 8th Air Force airfeilds and 4 former completely derelict 8th Air Force control towers have been laboriously renovated into memorial air museums at Bassingbourn, Cambridgeshire; Thorpe Abbotts, Norfolk; Framlingham, Suffolk and Seething, Norfolk.

For further information please contact:

Mr Brian Baldwin, 36 Fallowfield Walk, Hardwick Vale, Bury St Edmunds, Suffolk IP33 2QZ, England.

Buddies of the Ninth (BOTNA)

The Buddies of the Ninth Association was formed in the early 1980's by a group of English aviation enthusiasts who felt a particular affinity to the United States 9th Air Force in World War II. It has members on both sides of the Atlantic and one of its ideals is to encourage contact between 9th Air Force veterans and British people.

BOTNA meets every three months for discussions, film and video shows and general lecture evenings and all members receive a quarterly bulletin which is produced entirely by contributions from members. Airfield and group histories related by experts assist in the sharing of information about the 9th Air Force.

For further information please contact:

Mr Bob Mynn, The Dell, Kiln Hill, Ixworth, Suffolk IP31 2HW, England.

The FRIENDLY INVASION

Price £12.00

Available now from Terence Dalton Limited, Water Street, Lavenham, Sudbury, Suffolk Tel: (0787) 247572 and bookshops, stationers and Tourist Information Centres.

Roger A. Freeman

USAAF Reunion Classic Fighter Air Show

Sat 4th - Sun 5th July

In 1942 Duxford Airfield near Cambridge received one of the first US fighter groups to come to Britain, the 350th. For the rest of the war Duxford was home to American fighter squadrons of P-47 Thunderbolts and P-51 Mustangs.

Fifty years on, Duxford is now part of the Imperial War Museum and is home to 120 historic aircraft including the finest collection of American combat aircraft outside the US. Proud of its American connection, Duxford has a permanent exhibition devoted to the wartime US Eighth Air Force with a restored B-17 Flying Fortress as a centrepiece.

The 1992 Classic Fighter Air Show will take place at Duxford on Saturday 4 and Sunday 5 July. As 1992 will be the fiftieth anniversary of the arrival of US forces in Britain it is most appropriate that the weekend display will begin on the 4th of July - American Independence Day. The two day show will feature many of the American World War Two combat aircraft that helped the Allies achieve the final victory. His Royal Highness the Duke of York will attend the display on its opening day.

Visitors will be able to meet the men who made history as many hundreds of USAAF veterans are expected to attend.

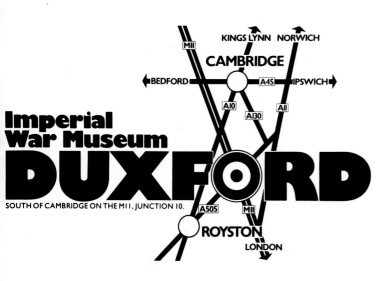

Imperial War Museum
DUXFORD
SOUTH OF CAMBRIDGE ON THE M11, JUNCTION 10.

The show will include:

- Red Arrows
- Mustangs
- Spitfires
- Hurricanes
- Messerschmitts
- Lancaster

- Flying Fortress
- Mosquito
- Hunter
- Phantom
- Tornado

Plus: Classic Cars, Big Bands, Market Stalls

Admission £8.00 Adults, £6.00 OAPs, £4.00 Children

Tickets are available in advance for this show:
£6.50 Adults, £4.50 OAPs, £3.00 Children

Special discount coach rates are available.

Further information available on 0223 835000

The East Anglia Tourist Board hope you will enjoy some of the events that have been organised to celebrate the 50th anniversary of the arrival of the USAAF in England. The Board have not organised any of the events themselves and cannot be held responsible for any inconvenience caused arising from errors, alterations or cancellations. It is advisable to telephone beforehand to check details. (Please note that the telephone numbers quoted are not necessarily those of the venue, but may be those of the event organiser).

If you are an American World War II veteran, please let people know you are coming beforehand to ensure a special welcome.

The dates of some events have been changed since the 2nd edition of 'Return to England'.

March

28th
The Glenn Miller Orchestra (UK) Ltd in Concert

Princess Theatre, Hunstanton, Norfolk Tel: 0485 532252

28th
The String of Pearls Orchestra in Concert

The Wyllyotts Centre, Potters Bar, Hertfordshire Tel: 0707 45005

April

4th
In the Mood

The Cressett, Peterborough, Cambridgeshire Tel: 0733 265705

The Herb Miller Orchestra in concert with the Kaye Sisters.

11th
The Syd Lawrence Orchestra in Concert

Alban Arena, St Albans, Hertfordshire Tel: 0727 861078

11th
Tribute Dance

St Ivo Recreation Centre, St Ives, Cambs Tel: 0480 64601

Dancing to The Sound Idea Big Band playing music by Glenn Miller and other big band leaders.

16th - 20th
Spring with the Big Band

Holiday Club Pontins, Pakefield, Lowestoft, Suffolk Tel: 0502 565117

A special tribute to the USAAF featuring Ray McVay Big Band, Andry Prior and the Nightowls, Vic Delaney, Herb Miller Orchestra and Todd Miller with the Joe Loss Orchestra. This is a special vacation including accommodation.

17th
In the Mood

Princes Theatre, Clacton-on-Sea, Essex Tel: 0255 423400

A tribute to the magic of Glenn Miller by the Herb Miller Orchestra, with the Kaye Sisters as special guests.

21st
Legends of Trad Jazz

Theatre Royal, Bury St Edmunds, Suffolk Tel: 0284 769505

A band of traditional jazz musicians under the direction of John Petters will play a mixture of traditional jazz music from around the world.

24th - 26th
The Syd Lawrence Orchestra Weekend

Holiday Club Pontins, Pakefield, Lowestoft, Suffolk Tel: 0502 565117

A special vacation including accommodation, featuring music by the Syd Lawrence Orchestra.

May

1st - 4th
Pakefield City Jazz Festival

Holiday Club Pontins, Pakefield, Lowestoft, Suffolk Tel: 0502 565117

A special vacation including accommodation, featuring jazz music.

2nd
The Glenn Miller Orchestra (UK) Ltd in Concert

The Brentwood International Centre, Brentwood, Essex Tel: 0277 262616

An Anglo-American Celebration.

2nd - 4th
International BMX Racing

Herlington Track, Orton Malborne, Peterborough Tel: 0733 222735

3rd
Annual Wing Parade and Families' Open Day

Carver Barracks, Wimbish, Saffron Walden, Essex Tel: 0799 521447

The HQ East Essex Wing ATC occupies a site on the former Debden airfield and their 1992 Open Day will emphasise the USAAF connection. A senior US personality will act as Reviewing Officer and there will be many items of interest on static display.

3rd

Historic Vehicle Run

Ipswich, Suffolk
Tel: 0473 624035

A rally of historic vehicles from Christchurch Park, Ipswich to the seafront at Felixstowe, including some American military vehicles.

3rd

'Spring Air Fete 92'

The Shuttleworth Collection, Biggleswade, Beds
Tel: 076 727 288

An action packed display including many of the collection's own historic aircraft plus participation by military aircraft and special attractions.

3rd

The Glenn Miller Orchestra (UK) Ltd in Concert

Regent Theatre,
Ipswich, Suffolk
Tel: 0473 281480

4th

The Syd Lawrence Orchestra in Concert

Spa Pavilion, Felixstowe, Suffolk
Tel: 0394 283303

4th

USAAF Reunion Amateur Golf Challenge

Quietwaters Golf & Country Club, near Maldon, Essex
Tel: 0702 480899

8th - 10th

Horham Weekend

Horham, Suffolk
Tel: 0379 384363

Rededication of the Eight Bells and Celebration Peals. This coincides with the return visit of the 95th Bomb Group.

9th

The Jonathan Wyatt Big Band in Concert

The Little Theatre,
Sheringham, Norfolk
Tel: 0263 823000

10th   3.30 pm

USAAF 50th Anniversary Commemorative Service

St Edmundsbury Cathedral, Bury St Edmunds, Suffolk
Tel: 0473 822922

A special service accompanied by a flypast and a street parade, including full RAF band. Admittance by ticket only (contact Jane Sullivan on above no.).

10th

Normandy Veterans Association Parade and Service

Norwich, Norfolk
Tel: 0603 627706

A parade through Norwich, service of thanksgiving and dedication at Norwich Cathedral to mark the 10th anniversary of the Normandy Veterans Association and a rally at St Andrews Hall, Norwich.

12th   2 pm

Memphis Belle

Cinema City, St Andrews Street, Norwich, Norfolk
Tel: 0603 622047

David Puttnam, the producer of the 'Memphis Belle', will introduce a special showing of the original technicolour documentary, (made as a British/American co-production in 1943 about the last mission over Germany of a Flying Fortress) and also the 1990 fictional feature film which takes the original documentary as its base.

14th - 16th

'Blitz'

Ipswich Regent, Suffolk
Tel: 0473 281480

Lionel Bart's musical about the Second World War, performed by the Ipswich Operatic and Dramatic Society.

15th - 17th

Return to Deopham Green

Great Ellingham Village Hall, nr Attleborough, Norfolk Tel: 0953 850897

An exhibition depicting the Americans' stay in Deopham Green during the Second World War. This coincides with the return visit of the 452nd Bomb Group.

16th   7.30 pm

Sounds of the Glenn Miller era by the Nick Ross Orchestra and Singers

West Cliff Theatre, Clacton-on-Sea, Essex
Tel: 0255 474000

Listen to music and songs of the 40s by the Nick Ross Orchestra and Singers.

16th

Village Reception in honour of 490th Bomb Group

Brome and Oakley, Suffolk
Tel: 0379 870288

Church service and garden party for returning veterans.

16th & 17th

Airshow Europe, incorporating Fighter Meet '92

North Weald Airfield, Epping, Essex
Tel: 081 866 9993

Airshow Europe 1992 will span 50 years of aviation and many performing aircraft will feature, among other things, the 50th anniversary of the American Eagle Squadron and the 8th and 9th Air Forces Reunion of 50 years. Flying will commence at 12.30 pm with non-stop flying displays until 6 pm. (Gates open at 9.30 am.)

17th

Annual Memorial Service

Cambridge American Military Cemetery, near Cambridge
Tel: 0954 210350

The moving annual service, including a fly-past, when veterans and their representatives lay wreaths to those who lost their lives.

19th - 21st

Film Festival

The Civic Theatre, Bedford
Tel: 0234 267422 ext 258

The Bedford Film Society will present a series of films to commemorate the American reunion.

23rd & 24th

Air Fete '92

RAF Mildenhall, Suffolk
Tel: 0638 513341

Hosted by the United States Air Force at the Headquarters of the US Third Air Force, the annual Air Fete is the largest air display organised by the military anywhere in the world and with an audience of over 300,000, the best attended in Britain. Air Fete '92 will commemorate the fiftieth anniversary of the USAAF in Britain.

23rd - 25th

10 am to 7 pm

Wormingford Flower Festival

St Andrews Church, Wormingford, Essex
Tel: 0206 241340

A three day flower festival which will include a tribute to the Americans' presence in East Anglia. Teas will be served in the local school.

24th

Opus One Big Band in Concert

beside Cliffs Pavilion, Southend-on-Sea, Essex
Tel: 0702 355166

An open air Glenn Miller style concert on the green.

24th & 25th

The Network SouthEast Southend Airshow

Southend-on-Sea, Essex
Tel: 0702 355166

Europe's greatest free airshow provides a spectacle of sound and colour in the skies above Southend-on-Sea. The opening day will be dedicated

to those men of courage who first arrived in East Anglia in 1942, with planes from this momentous era in history.

25th

USAAF Veterans' Day

The Muckleburgh Collection, Weybourne Military Camp (on coast road 5 miles west of Cromer), Norfolk
Tel: 026 370 210

One of the major events in the Veterans' Year. A large parade of war veterans with their standards, followed by a short open air service in memory of the fallen, which culminates in a special poppy drop from aircraft overhead and a march past with a senior USA General taking the salute. Other events include displays of working WWII tanks, an air display, military bands, a highland pipe band and many side displays. USA veterans welcome free of charge.

30th   7.30 pm

Glenn Miller Style Concert by the Opus One Big Band and featuring The Beverley Sisters

St Pauls Centre, Corn Exchange, Bedford
Tel: 0234 344813

The WRVS will be providing a display of wartime memorabilia within the St Pauls Centre to accompany this concert.

June

1st

USAAF Reunion Pro-Am Golf Tournament

Quietwaters Golf & Country Club, near Maldon, Essex
Tel: 0702 480899

A Pro-Am Golf Tournament giving amateurs the opportunity to compete alongside professional players.

6th & 7th

Cambridgeshire Festival of History and Aviation

Wood Green Animal Shelter, Godmanchester, Cambs
Tel: 0480 455521

Exhibition of aviation and historical items, talks and film shows and a flying display.

7th

'The Combat Aviation Display'

The Shuttleworth Collection, Biggleswade, Bedfordshire
Tel: 076 727 288 .

A special flying display with an Anglo-American theme featuring aircraft from World War II to the present day from both sides of the Atlantic.

7th

Belchamp St Paul Village Fete

Belchamp St Paul, Suffolk
Tel: 0787 237213

The 1992 fete will have a USAAF 50th anniversary theme and will include a display of military machinery.

8th - 13th

'Over Here ... Again!'

Riverside Theatre, Woodbridge, Suffolk
Tel: 0394 386965

A musical entertainment with music of the 40s by The Company of Four and a cast of 70.

10th - 13th

'Anything Goes'

Spa Pavilion, Felixstowe, Suffolk
Tel: 0394 283303

The Felixstowe Amateur Dramatic and Operatic Society perform Cole Porter's musical. A special welcome for USAAF veterans.

Events

13th
Sounds of the Glenn Miller era by the Nick Ross Orchestra and Singers

The Corn Exchange, Cambridge
Tel: 0223 357851

13th & 14th
International Air Tattoo

A&AEE Boscombe Down, Wiltshire
Tel: 0285 713300

The centrepiece of this air-show will be a salute to those members of the Mighty Eighth past and present and the organising team hopes to attract vintage warbirds and modern aircraft from all four corners of the globe.

14th
Amphibious Day at Fritton Lake and Country Park

near Great Yarmouth, Norfolk
Tel: 0493 488208

A celebration day at Fritton Lake, which was requisitioned by the War Office from 1942 for training with amphibious landing craft. The Catalina and DUKWs will be on the lake and there will be a barbecue as well as other attractions.

21st
The Syd Lawrence Orchestra in Concert

Princess Theatre, Hunstanton, Norfolk
Tel: 0485 532252

21st
Marriage Reunion Service

St Stephens Church, Norwich, Norfolk
Tel: 0603 615819

For those who were married in Norwich, with 'GI Brides' and their husbands especially welcome.

21st
RAF Swanton Morley Open Day

RAF Swanton Morley, Dereham, Norfolk
Tel: 0362 637291 ext 7196 or 7672

RAF station open day including a flying display and a station historical display which includes the involvement of the Americans during the war.

21st
USAAF Get-together

RAF Mildenhall, Suffolk
Tel: 0284 755217

A get-together with Suffolk County Royal British Legion - Suffolk County Women's Section, members of visiting groups and individuals from Stateside. This will include Royal British Legion standard bearers, a Remembrance parade followed by a thanksgiving service in a hangar. By kind permission of Colonel Blank.

24th - 27th
'Over Here ... Again!'

Spa Pavilion Theatre, Felixstowe, Suffolk
Tel: 0394 282126

A musical entertainment with music of the 40s by The Company of Four and a cast of 70.

26th
Dancing to the George Bradley Band

Nuthampstead, Hertfordshire
Tel: 0763 848744

Part of the celebrations for the return of the 398th Bomb Group.

26th
Commemorative Service

Peterborough Cathedral, Cambridgeshire
Tel: 0733 343342

27th & 28th
War, Men and Machinery and the Home Front

Anstey Village Hall, Anstey, near Buntingford, Hertfordshire Tel: 0763 848744

An exhibition which is on display for the return of the 398th Bomb Group

27th   7.30 pm
Dinner Dance

Airport Ambassador Hotel, Norwich Airport (previously Horsham St Faith), Norfolk
Tel: 0603 410544

Held by the Parachute Regimental Association with dancing to the String of Pearls Orchestra and a display by the Parachute Regiment Drums Platoon.

27th
RAF Honington 1992 Fete

The RAF pays tribute to the USAAF

RAF Honington, Bury St Edmunds, Suffolk
Tel: 0359 269561 ext 2758

An open day when American veterans will be welcomed with open arms. There will be a flying display, a static aircraft display, hangar exhibitions and much more.

27th
The Mainline Big Band in Concert

(by kind permission of Clifton Ibbott)

Milton House, Milton Ernest, Beds
Tel: 0234 215226

All proceeds to the North Beds Day Care Centre Appeal - Macmillan House.

28th
Banquet Dinner

Pembroke Hotel, Blackpool
Tel: Art Talbot on 0254 698929

Part of the celebrations for the BAD 2 Association Reunion in Blackpool.

28th

USAAF Reunion Day Fly-In

The Squadron,
North Weald Airfield,
Epping, Essex
Tel: 0378 824510

American built aeroplanes and military vehicles will be on static display and a special Reunion Lunch with WWII period band. (Advance tickets only for lunch). Squadron Museum aircraft also on display.

28th

Mid-Suffolk USAAF Memorial Service

Eye, Suffolk
Tel: 0359 259373

A procession through Eye accompanied by 5 bands, culminating in a memorial service at the Church of St Peter and St Paul.

July

1st - 14th

An Anglo-American Fortnight

East Anglia Region Best Western Hotels
Tel: 0603 787260

Featuring the best of traditional English cuisine and American wine and beers.

1st - 14th

40s American Nights

Pubs throughout Norfolk
Tel: 0603 426802

Organised by the Licenced Victuallers Association of Norwich and Norfolk.

3rd

Hangar Dance

(in aid of the Blenheim Restoration at Duxford)

Duxford Airfield, Cambs
Tel: 0799 513119

Dancing to the Opus One Big Band and the Beverley Sisters.

4th & 5th

USAAF Reunion Airshow - Duxford's Classic Fighter Display

Duxford Airfield,
Cambridgeshire
Tel: 0223 835000

This year's Show will have a USAAF 50th anniversary theme and will be one of the most exciting gatherings of flying military aircraft in Europe. The three hour display will feature World War II fighter aircraft, including Mustangs, Corsairs, Messerschmidts and many more. Duxford's own unrivalled collection of historic American combat aircraft will play a major part in the show with special exhibitions on the ground complementing the action in the air. There will be an area where veterans can rest and meet friends, old and new.

4th

'The Friendly Invasion' Dance

Norwich Sport Village,
Norwich, Norfolk
Tel: 0603 788898

Dancing to the Jonathan Wyatt Big Band and an American style celebration buffet.

4th

American Celebratory Dinner and 40s Night

Chilford Hall Barns,
Linton, Cambridgeshire
Tel: 0223 892641

Dancing to The Flying Colours Band and dining on American style food.

4th

American Extravaganza

The Corn Exchange,
Cambridge
Tel: 0223 357851

The Cambridge Orchestra playing American symphonic music including Rhapsody in Blue and other music by Gershwin.

4th

Barbecue and Dance (admittance by ticket only)

Thorpe Abbotts Airfield,
near Diss, Norfolk - Home of 100th Bomb Group
Tel: 0379 870837

Organised for the 100th Bomb Group who will be at Thorpe Abbotts holding their Reunion this weekend.

4th

Hangar Dance

Stansted, Essex
Tel: 076 387 612

Dancing to the Opus One Big Band.

4th

Fete, Barbecue and Glenn Miller style Dance

Stanway Village Hall and Playing Field, Colchester, Essex
Tel: 0206 330651

4th

Hangar Dance

(organised by Lions Club)
Fakenham Airfield, Norfolk
Tel: 0923 854363

Dancing to the String of Pearls Orchestra.

4th & 5th

Willingale Flower Festival

Willingale, Ongar, Essex
Tel: 0277 896353

A weekend of celebrations including church service in St Andrews Church (used by the Americans as their base church during the war), flower festival and village fete.

5th

The Syd Lawrence Orchestra in Concert

The Pavilion Theatre,
Cromer, Norfolk
Tel: 0263 511245

Events

5th

Public Open Day at Thorpe Abbotts

Thorpe Abbotts Airfield, near Diss, Norfolk - Home of 100th Bomb Group
Tel: 0379 870837

The 100th Bomb Group will be at Thorpe Abbotts holding a Reunion and will be pleased to meet members of the public.

6th

2.45 pm, 6.15 pm and 8.30 pm

USAAF Air Film Shows

Corn Exchange, Ipswich, Suffolk
Tel: 0473 742332

Special showings of archive aviation films from the USAAF and RAF, with all proceeds going to children's charities.

6th

USAAF Reunion Golf Challenge

Quietwaters Golf & Country Club, near Maldon, Essex
Tel: 0702 480899

Battle alongside professional golfers from the US Tour and the PGA European Tour and set your sights on winning one of the most prestigious one-day golf tournaments.

6th - 12th

USAAF Commemorative Convention

Emmanual College, Cambridge
Tel: 071 386 0266

A 6 day convention including a prestigious series of special briefings, social events and visits. Accommodation will be in Emmanual College and there will be a number of distinguished personalities present.

8th - 25th

2.30 pm to 7.30 pm

The Royal Tournament

Earls Court Exhibition Centre, London
Tel: 071 373 8141

A military pageant where the Forces join forces to make your day. This year it will be introduced by the RAF, telling the story of the heroes of the air and the display will include a glittering display of colour and jazz in a salute to mark the 50th anniversary of the arrival of the US forces in Britain.

10th

Commemorative Service

Norwich Cathedral, Norfolk
Tel: 0603 626290

17th

'Salute to Cole Porter'

Marina Theatre, Lowestoft, Suffolk
Tel: 0379 384505

A concert combining nostalgia with excellence with The London Sinfonietta, a top British orchestra, performing some of America's greatest popular music including many Cole Porter classics.

17th - 19th

Weeting Steam Rally

Weeting, Suffolk
Tel: 0842 810317

A 3 day steam rally with approximately 100 traction engines, most of which are in working order and can be seen ploughing, woodsawing, timber loading etc. A large display of 40s military vehicles, vintage tractors, vintage and veteran cars. There will also be a special '50 years of Anglo-American Friendship' exhibition.

18th

Commemorative Service

Chelmsford Cathedral, Essex
Tel: 0245 263660

24th

'Hooked on Classics' featuring 'Hooked on the USA'

Western Esplanade, Southend-on-Sea, Essex
Tel: 0702 355166

A pops classic concert by the Royal Philharmonic Orchestra conducted by Louis Clark.

25th

Veterans' Day

390th Bomb Group Museum, Parham, Suffolk
Tel: 0379 898085

An open day with a military vehicle display and an extra special welcome for returning veterans.

25th

BBC Radio Big Band Concert

Western Esplanade, Southend-on-Sea, Essex
Tel: 0702 355166

The BBC augmented Radio Big Band will recreate the Glenn Miller Army Air Force Orchestra.

26th

Open Day in Aid of SSAFA by kind permission of Mr & Mrs Ward Thomas

Horham Hall, near Thaxted, Essex
Tel: 0371 830389

House and garden open and teas served with a special welcome for returning veterans.

29th

Sandringham Flower Show

Sandringham Park, Norfolk
Tel: 0485 540575

The magnificent annual flower show held at Sandringham Park which is owned by HRH Queen Elizabeth II.

August

2nd

Military Vehicle Display

Duxford Airfield, Cambridgeshire
Tel: 0223 835000

A gathering of historic military vehicles.

2nd

'Summer Air Fete'

The Shuttleworth Collection, Biggleswade, Beds
Tel: 076 727 288

Combining military and civil aircraft in a varied programme with amusing as well as fascinating displays. A family day out with enough interest to satisfy the enthusiast as well.

3rd

USAAF Reunion Celebrity-Am Tournament

Quietwaters Golf & Country Club, near Maldon, Essex.
Tel: 0702 480899

A chance to compete at golf alongside a celebrity.

4th   8 pm

Stars and Stripes Concert

The Thursford Collection, Thursford, Norfolk
Tel: 0328 878477

A two hour concert featuring much American music and starring Robert Wolfe at the famous Thursford Wurlitzer cinema organ.

7th

An American Prom

Snape Maltings, Aldeburgh, Suffolk
Tel: 0800 585 789

A programme of American music by the City of London Sinfonia. Part of the British Telecom Snape Proms.

8th

The Glenn Miller Orchestra (UK) Ltd in Concert

Spa Pavilion Theatre, Felixstowe, Suffolk
Tel: 0394 283303

13th & 14th

The Walgrave Village Festival

Walgrave, Northamptonshire
Tel: 0604 781781

A village festival with a Back to the 40s theme, including a military vehicle display, exhibitions, craft market and an Officers' Mess Night.

14th   7.30 pm

40s Nite

Woolpack Hotel, Islip, Northamptonshire
Tel: 08012 2578
(after May 1992 0832 732578)

Parade of USA vehicles through Thrapston High Street into Islip, led by Thrapston Town Band, which will play in Woolpack car park until 8.30 pm. Supper (bangers and mash) and dance at 8.30 pm in Woolpack Restaurant. (Tickets to be purchased in advance)

14th

Glenn Miller style dance

The George Hotel, Kettering, Northamptonshire
Tel: 0536 518620

Dancing to 'Fanfare' 18 piece band and readings from 'Piggy in the Middle' a wartime love story by Paula McKay.

15th

Rothwell Festival

Rothwell, Northamptonshire
Tel: 0536 710799

A festival with 40s street market and band for dancing in the square.

15th & 16th

American Weekend in Braintree

Braintree, Essex
Tel: 0376 552525 ext 2331

Memorial service and dedication for US 12th Evacuation and 121st Station Hospital - White Court, Black Notley.

Historic vehicle drive past and rally.

Military vehicle rally and flypast with militaria market and show.

Ivy Benson and 1940s dance band at Towerlands, with American wartime vehicles and swing band nostalgia.

15th & 16th

American Civil War Re-enactment

Sulgrave Manor, Sulgrave, Northants Tel: 029 576 205

16th   11.30 am

50th Anniversary Memorial Service

Geddington Road, Grafton Underwood, Northants
Tel: 0536 78249

A special memorial service with flypast beside the 384th Bomb Group Memorial. Any organisation wishing to place a wreath during the service would be most welcome.

16th   11 am to 5 pm

Eighth Air Force Equipment exhibition

Grafton Underwood Village Hall, Northamptonshire
Tel: 0536 78249

An exhibition consisting of a wide variety of exhibits including settings of a 'barracks' cum 'briefing room' cum 'station office'.

16th

Kettering Vintage & Classic Car Show with an American Theme

Meadow Road, Kettering, Northamptonshire
Tel: 0536 518747

This year's event, depicting motoring heritage from 1903 to 1978, will have a special American theme.

18th - 20th

10 am to 3 pm

40s Childrens' Activity Days

Holdenby House Gardens, Holdenby, Northants
Tel: 0604 770074

For children aged 4 to 13. Children to arrive with name tag as an evacuee. Ration books will be issued and children will exchange coupons for lunch etc. Games will be as of the 'War Years'. Anderson shelter and air raid sirens will be experienced.

21st - 23rd

40s Weekend at Boughton House

Boughton House, Kettering, Northants
Tel: 0536 515731

Friday night - 'Wartime Palais Nite' including light wartime refreshments.

Saturday night - Open air Glenn Miller style concert.

Sunday night - Officers' Mess Dinner.

Throughout the weekend there will be an exhibition of World War II memorabilia.

23rd

Cromer Airshow

Northrepps Air Field, near Cromer, Norfolk
Tel: 0263 513015

An airshow run in conjunction with the Barnstormer Flying Circus, including 40s primary trainer aircraft with US Steermans and Tiger Moths. There will also be a military vehicle display.

28th

Hangar Dance

Thurleigh Airfield, Bedfordshire
Tel: 0234 708715 (evenings and weekends)

Dancing to the Herb Miller Orchestra as part of the celebrations for the return of the 306th Bomb Group.

29th

Church Concert

St Michael's Church Aylsham, Norfolk
Tel: 0263 87829

A concert with an American theme featuring the Fine Arts Brass and the Ionian Singers.

30th & 31st

Eye Show

Eye Showground, Suffolk
Tel: 0379 870224

A family weekend including a USAAF display of memorabilia and photographs, vintage vehicles and other military equipment.

September

1st   8 pm

American Patrol Concert

Thursford Collection, Thursford, Norfolk
Tel: 0328 878477

A two hour concert featuring much American music and starring Robert Wolfe at the famous Thursford Wurlitzer cinema organ.

5th

40s Night

(in aid of Sue Ryder Homes)

Perkins Engines, Peterborough
Tel: 0733 60222

Dancing to the Johnny Harris Orchestra and many celebrities in a simulated hangar. Dress 40s style.

6th

2nd Air Division 50th Anniversary Celebratory Open Day

USAAF Liberator base, Station 146, Seething, Norfolk.
Tel: 0508 50787

A special open day at the control tower with personal diaries, memorabilia and hundreds of photographs on display. There will be a large static display of US service aircraft from the Second World War and military vehicles. The 2nd Air Division Memorial Library will be providing an exhibition of aviation art and photographs.

On 4th, 5th & 6th visitors are especially welcome to visit the Flower Festival at St Margarets and St Remigiues Church, Seething, the Art and Craft Exhibition and flower display at St Peters Church, Mundham and an exhibition of the history of the villages of Mundham and Seething at Seething Village Hall.

6th

Open Day to celebrate Return to England

Somerleyton Hall and Gardens, Somerleyton, Lowestoft, Suffolk
Tel: 0502 730224

A special open day including an American supper (tickets by advance only) and an open air service.

6th

'The Shuttleworth Pageant'

The Shuttleworth Collection, Biggleswade, Beds
Tel: 076 727288

A vintage air display with historic and current long serving aircraft from the collection, from military sources and other collections. A historic vehicle parade will precede the flying display.

Events

Events

7th 2.45 pm

USAAF Air Film Show

Corn Exchange, Ipswich,
Suffolk
Tel: 0473 742332

A special showing of archive
aviation films from the
USAAF and RAF. All proceeds
go to children's charities.

7th

**USAAF Reunion
Amateur Golf Challenge**

Quietwaters Golf & Country
Club, near Maldon, Essex.
Tel: 0702 480899

10th 2.30 pm

Commemorative Service

Ely Cathedral,
Ely, Cambridgeshire
Tel: 0353 667735

For the crews who returned,
the cathedral landmark
symbolised home.

11th - 13th

**Fall of Eagles Memorial
Weekend**

Staplehurst, Kent
Tel: 0622 686342

A special weekend including
a memorial service, visit to
the airfields and the dedication of a new memorial to the
363rd Fighter Group and the
126th RCAF Wing.

12th

Hangar Dance

Hangar 520, RAF Alconbury,
Cambs
Tel: 0480 823351

Dancing to the Mainline Big
Band.

13th

Duxford '92 Flying Day

Duxford Airfield, Cambs
Tel: 0223 835000

Duxford's annual air display
will include a variety of the
finest historic and modern
aircraft, both civil and military, with contributions from
many of the top aerobatic
pilots in a three hour air show.

20th - 26th

**King's Lynn USAAF
Week**

King's Lynn,
Norfolk
Tel: 0485 532516

A special week including
events such as a big band
concert, dance and exhibition.

26th

**Sounds of the Glenn
Miller era by The Nick
Ross Orchestra and
Singers**

Watersmeet Theatre,
Rickmansworth,
Hertfordshire
Tel: 0923 896484

26th - 2nd October

**Debden Celebration
Week**

Debden, nr Saffron Walden,
Essex
Tel: 0799 40866

A week of activities including an air show, a military
vehicle display and reunion
celebrations.

October

5th

**USAAF Reunion
Amateur Golf Challenge**

Quietwaters Golf & Country
Club, near Maldon, Essex
Tel: 0702 480899

6th - 11th

Big Band Special

Holiday Club Pontins,
Pakefield, Lowestoft,
Suffolk
Tel: 0502 565117

Featuring the orchestras of
Syd Lawrence, Ray McVay
and Herb Miller in a special
tribute to Big Bands.

(This is a special vacation
including accommodation).

8th - 18th

**Norfolk and Norwich
Festival**

Norwich, Norfolk
Tel: 0603 614921

Britain's second oldest
festival will present a series
of special American events
over the weekend of 10th to
12th October, including an
American Early Music
Group at Blackfriars Hall on
11th and 'A Broadway
Melody' with songs and
music from popular Broadway
shows down the years, with
a full jazz band accompani-
ment, at St Andrews Hall on
12th. Also an American-
style brunch, a debate on
Columbus, readings, films
and special events for
children.

16th - 17th

**Todd Miller with the Joe
Loss Orchestra**

Holiday Club Pontins,
Pakefield, Lowestoft, Suffolk
Tel: 0502 565711

A special vacation including
accommodation.

November

13th

**Sounds of the Glenn
Miller era by the Nick
Ross Orchestra and
Singers**

Corn Exchange, Ipswich,
Suffolk Tel: 0473 215544

25th

**Sounds of the Glenn
Miller era by the Nick
Ross Orchestra and
Singers**

Theatre Royal,
Bury St Edmunds, Suffolk
Tel: 0284 769505/755469

21st August 1991 - July 1992
'The Grand Alliance'

Royal Air Force Museum,
Hendon, London
Tel: 081 205 2266

A dedicated art exhibition to commemorate the events of December 1941 and the entry of the USA into the war, including original work from British and American artists.

December 1991 - July 1992
'Pilot Officer Prune'

Royal Air Force Museum,
Hendon, London
Tel: 081 205 2266

Remember the exploits of 'Prune' and his contribution to the Allied efforts? This exhibition features the original mannequins created by Bill Hooper, Prune's originator, plus a number of cartoons and drawings.

April & May
'Rivenhall Airfield in World War II'

Feering and Kelvedon Local History Museum, Essex
Tel: 0376 70307

An exhibition of photographs, memorabilia etc, depicting life on the airfield during the war.

Easter - September
8th Air Force Exhibition

Woolpit Bygones Museum,
Woolpit, Suffolk
Tel: 0359 40822

An exhibition including photographs, models, maps and memorabilia showing all aspects of life on Great Ashfield, Rattlesden and Rougham airfields during the war.

17th April - 24th December
'The 8th Air Force in and around Peterborough'

Peterborough Museum,
Priestgate, Peterborough
Tel: 0733 343329

An exhibition of models, photographs, diorama, pictures and memorabilia of the airfields around Peterborough, including Glatton and Polebrook.

April - October
'Return to East Anglia 1992'

Long Shop Museum,
Leiston, Suffolk
Tel: 0728 832189

A special exhibition as a salute to the 357th Fighter Group - 'The Yoxford Boys'

13th - 25th April
'USAAF 1942-1992'

The Frame Workshop,
22 St Nicholas St, Ipswich
Tel: 0473 219875

An American season of original paintings and limited edition prints. Print samples available for viewing from April to September and individual commissions taken.

18th April - 16th May
'Memories of the Mighty Eighth'

Royston Museum, Royston,
Hertfordshire
Tel: 0763 242587

War, men and machines and the home front of Memphis Belle country.

18th April - 1st November
'The Home Front and 50 years of US presence'

Woodbridge Museum,
Woodbridge, Suffolk
Tel: 0394 382178

A special exhibition to mark 50 years of presence of the US allies. Memorabilia and photographs from Debach and Martlesham Heath airfields and the Woodbridge area.

6th May - 16th August
'Suffolk Summer - Wartime Memories'

Moyse's Hall Museum,
Bury St Edmunds, Suffolk
Tel: 0284 757072

Follow the journey of discovery made by one American, John Appleby, who was stationed here and fell in love with the place and its people.

May - September
Suffolk's Travelling Exhibition

Libraries in Suffolk
Tel: 0473 264566

A travelling exhibition of contemporary photographs, newspaper cuttings and equipment. Visiting libraries throughout Suffolk.

May to August
'The 8th and 9th Air Forces at Wormingford'

Wormingford Village Hall,
Wormingford, Essex
Tel: 0787 228024 (please telephone to arrange access)

A display of local photographs taken when the 8th and 9th were at Wormingford, along with details of their history.

May - September
'Pilgrims and Adventurers'

Cressing Temple Barns,
nr Witham, Essex
Tel: 0376 84903

An exhibition about Essex's part in the making of the United States.

16th May - 2nd August
'The American Air Force in Bedford'

The Bedford Museum, Bedford
Tel: 0234 533323

Photographs, memorabilia and uniforms telling the story of the 306th Bomb Group's presence at Thurleigh and Bedford.

16th - 23rd May
An Aeronautical Art Exhibition

Rugby Library, Warwickshire
Tel: 0788 570054

An exhibition of modern day paintings of subjects relating to aviation, including aeroplanes, men and women, factories, airfields, actions and paraphernalia.

Exhibitions

23rd May - 5th July

'At Home - East Anglia During the War'

Museum of East Anglian Life, Stowmarket, Suffolk
Tel: 0449 612229

An exhibition looking at the lives of those whose contribution to the war effort came from the Home Front.

June - September

Second World War Exhibition

Landguard Fort Museum, Felixstowe, Suffolk
Tel: 0394 286403

An exhibition on the Second World War presented by the Felixstowe History and Museum Society, including photographs and memorabilia etc. (Open Wed, Thur & Sun pm or by appointment).

2nd June - 4th July

'The American West'

The Bedford Central Library, Bedford
Tel: 0234 268840

An exhibition of the paintings of Albert R Tilburne 1887-1965. To coincide with the exhibition there will be a 4th July celebration with music and poetry.

22nd June - 11th July

50th Anniversary Book Exhibition

Heffers Bookshop, 20 Trinity St, Cambridge
Tel: 0223 358351

An exhibition of relevant books and memorabilia.

30th June and throughout July

Tribute Art Exhibition

The Coach House Gallery, Old Costessey, Norwich
Tel: 0603 662080

A tribute art exhibition featuring scenes and landmarks associated with the bases in Norfolk that were used by the USAAF.

Throughout July

Tribute Art Exhibition

Trading Places Gallery, Ware, Hertfordshire
Tel: 0920 469620

A tribute art exhibition featuring scenes and landmarks associated with the bases in Bedfordshire, Cambridgeshire, East Essex and Hertfordshire that were used by the USAAF.

18th July - 25th October

'North Weald and the Allies'

Epping Forest District Museum, Waltham Abbey, Essex
Tel: 0992 716882

An exhibition of the sights and sounds of historic North Weald Aerodrome during the Second World War, with photographs, memorabilia and historic room recreations. It will highlight the contribution of the Allied Powers and life on the Home Front.

July and August

'In a Familiar Land'

The Haste Gallery, Ipswich, Suffolk
Tel: 0473 258429

A tribute art exhibition featuring landscape paintings for sale of areas around airfields in Suffolk. Official opening 1st July.

1st - 29th August

'Memories of the Mighty Eighth'

Letchworth Museum, Letchworth, Herts
Tel: 0462 685647

War, men and machines and the home front of Memphis Belle country.

2nd August - 13th September

'Wartime Railways'

(part of the Leighton Buzzard Steam Festival)

Leighton Buzzard Railway, Bedfordshire
Tel: 0525 373888

Part of the display will feature photographs of the railway during the wartime era. Over the August Bank Holiday weekend, there will be a special display depicting USAAF activities in the area.

10th - 29th August

'USAAF 1942-1992'

The Frame Workshop, 22 St Nicholas St, Ipswich
Tel: 0473 219875

An American season of original paintings and limited edition prints. Print samples available for viewing from April to September and individual commissions taken.

14th - 29th August

Exhibition by Kettering Aircraft Research Group

Alfred East Gallery, Kettering, Northamptonshire
Tel: 0536 514849

As part of the exhibition, on 15th August, at 1 pm there will be readings from 'Piggy in the Middle', a love story set in wartime Kettering, by Paula McKay.

21st - 23rd August

World War II Exhibition

Boughton House, nr Kettering, Northamptonshire
Tel: 0536 515731

An exhibition of memorabilia and photographs depicting the war years in Northamptonshire.

19th December, 1992 - 17th January, 1993

'Memories of the Mighty Eighth'

Hitchin Museum, Hitchin, Herts
Tel: 0462 434476

War, men and machines and the home front of Memphis Belle country.

2nd Air Division Memorial Library

Bethel Street, Norwich, Norfolk

Tel: 0603 223852

In the Central Library at Norwich, Norfolk, England there is a unique memorial to over 6,400 Americans of the 2nd Air Division, USAAF who did not return to their homeland.

The Room in the Norwich Central Library containing the Roll of Honor with books and other material on American culture and with four Branch Library Collections in Norfolk, forms part of the 2nd Air Division Memorial.

Other parts of the memorial comprise archives and historic papers for research, films, video and educational activities. This resource has been established to encourage better understanding of our friends in the United States of America and of that great country.

In the words inscribed on the memorial bookplate, on the wooden screen by the Roll of Honor and the memorial garden in the Library courtyard, it is: "In memory of those Americans who, flying from bases in these parts, gave their lives defending freedom. 1941-1945".

The idea of the Memorial was born in the hearts and minds of able, brave and intelligent Americans out of their experience of living, working and fighting in England during World War 2. That experience had been shared with us, a people of another country, who spoke the same language and with whom an affinity developed through the stresses and strains of war.

In the words of Brig Gen Milton W Arnold (USAAF) - a Founder Governor of the Trust:

"It is a tangible and permanent expression of the lasting friendship between our two nations and between ourselves as individual Americans and the individual English men and women in this community."

Photograph shows the 2nd Air Division Memorial Library at Norwich.

Cambridge American Cemetery & Memorial

Madingley, Cambs Tel: 0954 210350

The Cambridge American Cemetery and Memorial is one of 14 permanent American WWII military cemetery memorials erected on foreign soil by the American Battle Monuments Commission. It was established as a temporary military cemetery in 1943 on land donated by the University of Cambridge and the site was later selected as the only permanent American WWII military cemetery in the British Isles.

3,812 American War Dead are buried here in graves laid out in a fan shape arrangement sweeping widely across beautifully maintained lawns covering an area of 30.5 acres.

The Memorial structure takes the form of a large museum room and a small devotional chapel, the outstanding feature of which is an impressive map which indicates the principal sea routes across the Atlantic and the types of naval and commercial craft which bore men and munitions to Europe from the United States. It also recalls the aircraft which operated in the anti-submarine campaign. The continuous air assaults by the US and Royal Air Forces over Europe are also depicted.

Leading up to the Memorial is the Wall of the Missing. This is 472 feet in length and records the names and particulars of 5,126 Americans missing in action or lost or buried at sea. 3,524 of these were members of the United States Army Air Forces who died during World War II.

Visitors wishing to locate the grave of a missing person, have simply to give the name and if possible the bomber or fighter group of that person and the Superintendent will be happy to take them to the grave concerned.

Memorials

**1st SAD
(Honington, Suffolk)**

Memorial at RAF airfield dedicated 26.9.1987.

**2nd Air Division
(Norwich, Norfolk)**

Memorial library and fountain.

**2nd Air Division HQ
(Ketteringham Hall,
Norfolk)**

Plaque in hall grounds and plate on organ in St Peters Church, Ketteringham.

**2nd Air Division
(Attleborough Library,
Norfolk)**

Plaque to 2nd Combat Wing.

**2nd Air Division
(East Dereham Library,
Norfolk)**

Plaque to 14th Combat Wing.

**2nd Air Division
(Long Stratton Library,
Norfolk)**

Plaque to 20th Combat Wing.

**2nd Air Division
(Sprowston Library,
Norfolk)**

Plaque to 96th Combat Wing.

**2nd BAD
(Warton, Lancashire)**

Plaque at BAc factory entrance, memorial and playing field at Freckleton village.

**3rd SAD
(Watton, Norfolk)**

Memorial in Griston churchyard, plaques and flag in church.

**3rd Air Division HQ
(Elveden Hall, Suffolk)**

Fine stained glass window in village church.

**4FG
(Debden, Essex)**

Memorial on old base (now Carver Army Barracks) dedicated 11.7.1981.

**5ERS/56FG/489BG
(Halesworth, Suffolk)**

Drop tank memorial to units located on airfield and plaque to all USAAF units in Holton church.

**7th Photo Group
(Mount Farm, Oxfordshire)**

Propellor memorial in Beringsfield village dedicated 25.5.1985. Memorial in Dorchester Abbey grounds.

Plaque at base of village sign at Foulsham, Norfolk.

**20FG/Allied squadrons
(King's Cliffe, Northants)**

Memorial at old airfield dedicated 10.12.1986.

**25BG
(Watton, Norfolk)**

Memorial at old base entrance, dedicated 9.6.1984.

**31FG
(Westhampnett, Sussex)**

Memorial on old airfield, dedicated 26.9.1987.

**34BG
(Mendlesham, Suffolk)**

Memorial with bronze plaque depicting B-17 pilot, on A140 opposite airfield.

**44BG
(Shipdham, Norfolk)**

Memorial in churchyard and on old airfield, dedicated 24.9.1988.

**50/52 Troop Carrier
Wings (Cottesmore,
Leicestershire)**

Memorial at entrance to RAF Cottesmore dedicated 1945.

**55FG
(Wormingford, Essex)**

Memorial photograph in Crown Public House.

56FG (see 5ERS)

**61TCG (Barkston Heath,
Lincolnshire)**

Two memorial plaques at Lincolnshire Police HQ at Nettleham.

**65 Fighter Wing HQ
(Saffron Walden, Essex)**

Memorial apse and Anglo-American playing field.

**78FG
(Duxford,
Cambridgeshire)**

Memorial stone located at main entrance to airfield.

8th Air Force memorial room within museum.

**91BG
(Bassingbourn,
Cambridgeshire)**

B-17 propellor memorial at main entrance to old airfield (now Army Barracks) dedicated 23.5.1978. Flower garden and memorial in Royston, dedicated July 1989. Plaque in council offices.

**92BG
(Podington, Bedfordshire)**

Restored church organ dedicated 18.5.1985 and propellor memorial.

**93BG
(Hardwick, Norfolk)**

Memorial stone on airfield, dedicated May 1987. Plaque in Topcroft church.

**94BG
(Bury St Edmunds,
Suffolk)**

Memorial (dated 15.10.77, when the money was raised) dedicated 5.10.1978.

Seat (made from B-17) within the John Appleby Rose Garden.

**95BG
(Horham, Suffolk)**

Memorial in village dedicated 19.9.1981. Flag in Stradbroke church dedicated November 1981 (replaces original that was presented in 1945 and stolen from the church). Church bells to be rededicated in 1992.

**96BG
(Snetterton Heath, Norfolk)**

Stained glass window in Quidenham church, dedicated in 1944 also plaque/flags in church. Memorial museum at old hospital site at Eccles Hall School.

**100BG
(Thorpe Abbotts, Norfolk)**

Memorial tower museum and plaques dedicated 25.5.1981.

**305BG
(Chelveston, Northamptonshire)**

Plaque on restored church tower dedicated 24.9.1980.

**306BG
(Thurleigh, Bedfordshire)**

Memorial at airfield, dedicated 5.10.1982.

**314TCG
(Saltby, Leicestershire)**

Plaque in Sproxton village church (once at Crown Inn, Sproxton) dedicated, 3.8.1970.

**315TCG
(Spanhoe, Northamptonshire)**

Memorial obelisk at old airfield entrance, dedicated in 1983. Small memorial in Tinwell church to crash victims.

**322BG
(Great Saling/
Andrewsfield, Essex)**

Memorial stone in village to 819th AAF Engineers.

**323BG
(Earls Colne, Essex)**

Museum dedicated to 9th Air Force on old airfield.

Memorial planned for 1992 at nearby Marks Hall.

**339FG
(Fowlmere, Cambridgeshire)**

Memorial on old airfield and plaque in village school dedicated 20.9.1986.

**344BG
(Stansted, Essex)**

Plaque to 344th and engineers that built the airfield, in Bishops Stortford History Museum, dedicated May 1989.

**351FG
(Polebrook, Northamptonshire)**

Memorial on airfield, site of old runway, dedicated June 1981.

**352FG
(Bodney, Norfolk)**

Memorial stone on old airfield, dedicated 9.7.1983.

**353FG
(Metfield, Suffolk)**

Plaque to be dedicated in church in 1992.

**353FG
(Raydon, Suffolk)**

New church doors dedicated 25.8.1984.

**354FG
(Boxted, Essex)**

Plans for a plaque.

**355FG
(Steeple Morden, Cambridgeshire)**

Propellor memorial at airfield.

**356FG
(Martlesham Heath, Suffolk)**

Memorial on old airfield.

**357FG
(Leiston, Suffolk)**

Plaque on wall of town council house, dedicated 8.5.1980.

**359FG
(East Wretham, Norfolk)**

Memorial plaque in churchyard at East Wretham and plaque in Thetford town square dedicated 3.8.1985.

**361FG
(Little Walden, Essex)**

Plaque in restored control tower, dedicated June 1987.

**361FG
(Bottisham, Cambridgeshire)**

Plaque in Holy Trinity Church dedicated 17.6.1984 and memorial stone in village dedicated 16.10.1988.

**362FG
(Wormingford, Essex)**

Plaque at Crown Inn. New memorial planned for 1992.

**362FG
(Ashford, Kent)**

Memorial steps at Bedlam Lane, Egerton, Kent.

**364FG
(Honington, Suffolk)**

Memorial seat in rose garden at Bury St Edmunds.

Memorial on RAF airfield dedicated in 1990.

**379BG
(Kimbolton, Northamptonshire)**

Memorial on airfield dedicated 19.8.1989. Plaque and memorial book in village church.

**381BG
(Ridgewell, Essex)**

Memorial, close to Yeldham village, dedicated 28.8.1982. Memorial plaque in Ashen church dated 1986.

**384BG
(Grafton Underwood, Northamptonshire)**

Memorial located at old airfield. Fine stained glass window in village church dedicated May 1983.

**385BG
(Great Ashfield, Suffolk)**

Plaque in village churchyard and memorial and roll of honor within church.

**386BG
(Great Dunmow, Essex)**

Memorial column situated at old Strood Hall entrance to base. Fine stained glass windows in Little Easton church dedicated 5.10.1990.

Memorials

388BG
(Knettishall, Suffolk)

Fine memorial at old entrance to base in village of Coney Weston, dedicated 17.5.1986.

389BG
(Hethel, Norfolk)

Memorial room in original control tower. Also memorial tablet at Carlton Rode church to crew from 389th who crashed on 21.11.44.

390BG
(Framlingham/Parham, Suffolk)

Original control tower museum and plaque dedicated May 1981.

391BG
(Matching Green, Essex)

Two plaques in church, one dated September 1981.

392BG
(Wendling, Norfolk)

Memorial obelisk, dedicated September 1945 and resited July 1989.

394BG
(Boreham, Essex)

Memorial column at old entrance to airfield, erected 5.6.48.

48 star flag in St Andrews Church.

New memorial stone at airfield dedicated in 1991.

397BG
(Rivenhall, Essex)

Memorial plaques held by Marconi Co in Chelmsford. One plaque dedicated 17.6.1984.

398BG
(Nuthampstead, Hertfordshire)

Monument stone erected in village, dedicated September 1982. Plaques in Woodman Public House.

401BG
(Deenethorpe, Northamptonshire)

Memorial stained glass window, dedicated in 1945, flag and plaques in St Mary's Church, Weldon. Centre panels of window are from old base chapel.

Memorial at airfield dedicated 16.9.1989.

Church bell donated in 1975.

406 Bomb Squadron
(Cheddington, Buckinghamshire)

Memorial at old base entrance incorporates original runway light which is lit on special occasions - dedicated October 1982.

406FG
(Ashford, Kent)

Plaque.

409BG
(Little Walden, Essex)

Plaque in restored control tower dedicated in 1985.

410BG
(Gosfield, Essex)

New granite memorial with plaque dedicated May 1991.

434TCG and 442TCG
(Fulbeck, Lincs)

Rose bush memorial in churchyard presented by 931st Air Refuelling Group - lineal descendant of 434TCG - in 1978.

Three pictorial plaques in village hall.

436TCG
(Membury, Berkshire)

Plaque in local museum.

437TCG
(Ramsbury, Wiltshire)

Plaque in village church.

442TCG
(Fulbeck, Lincs)

See 434TCG.

445BG
(Tibenham, Norfolk)

Memorial on old airfield (site of old control tower), dedi-

cated 25.5.1987. Plaque in village church.

446BG
(Bungay/Flixton, Suffolk)

Oak wood church gates at Flixton presented in 1945 and re-dedicated 1987, memorial seat and roll of honor. Plaque in Bungay Community Centre dedicated May 1983.

Additional plaque on airfield dedicated 20.5.1974.

447BG
(Rattlesden, Suffolk)

Memorial at old airfield, dedicated 3.6.1984.

448BG
(Seething, Norfolk)

Memorials in village church and on airfield, dedicated 6.6.1984. Restored control tower museum and memorial.

452BG
(Deopham Green, Norfolk)

Memorial plaque dedicated 11.5.1985 and flag at Hingham church. (Original bronze plaque dedicated in May 1979 has been relocated at Attleborough railway station).

Lincoln Hall displays new plaque dedicated August 1979, presented by 452nd Air Refuelling Wing USAF.

453BG
(Old Buckenham, Norfolk)

Village hall extension memorial containing plaque. Memorial stone on old airfield, dedicated 29.7.1990.

457BG
(Glatton, Cambridgeshire)

Memorial in Conington churchyard dedicated in 1984.

458BG
(Horsham St Faith, Norfolk)

Plaque and small museum in Norwich airport terminal.

466BG
(Attlebridge, Norfolk)

Village sign at Weston Long-ville, Norfolk dedicated 27.8.1977. Memorial plaque and flag in church dedicated July 1990.

New memorial scheduled for dedication at Attlebridge in 1992.

467BG
(Rackheath, Norfolk)

Village sign, plaque and seat dedicated 8.10.1983. Memorial on old airfield 'Liberator Road', dedicated 29.7.1990.

479FG
(Wattisham, Suffolk)

Plaque in RAF Station HQ presented October 1988.

486BG
(Sudbury, Suffolk)

Plaque on town hall dedicated 2.8.1945. Memorial at St Gregory's church dedicated 4.7.1987. Memorial at old airfield entrance dedicated 26.7.1986.

487BG
(Lavenham, Suffolk)

Plaque in market place dedicated August 1970. Plaque and flag in church. Plaque on original control tower dedicated 10.5.1986.

489BG
(Halesworth, Suffolk)

See 5ERS. Also memorial stone dedicated May 1983 and small park dedicated to 489th.

490BG
(Eye, Suffolk)

Tiled memorial bus stop, designed like a well in Brome village dedicated 25.8.1984.

491BG
(Metfield, Suffolk)

Plaque to be dedicated in church in 1992.

491BG/492BG
(North Pickenham, Norfolk)

Memorial at old airfield, seat in Swaffham Market Place and memorial clock in North Pickenham church, dedicated July 1990.

492BG/801BG
(Harrington, Northamptonshire)

Memorial to the 'Carpetbag-gers' on old airfield. Tablet in Topcroft church.

493BG
(Debach, Suffolk)

Flags and plaque in Clopton church; draped flag above plaque presented in 1945 from old base.

Village sign memorial with plaque erected in 1991.

496 Fighter Training Group
(Goxhill, Lincolnshire)

P-38 propellor memorial on airfield, dedicated 9.9.1984.

Additional memorials:

Bedford Corn Exchange, Memorial plaque to the late Glenn Miller (AAF Band).

Wycombe Abbey School, Buckinghamshire, 8th Air Force HQ - Plaque to 'Pine-tree'.

Bushy Park, Teddington, Middlesex, USAAF HQ - Plaque to USAAF.

St Clement Danes Church, London, USAF Shrine, church organ memorial and book of remembrance.

St Pauls Cathedral, London, US Memorial chapel - Stained glass window memorial.

Grosvenor Square, London, American Eagle Squadron memorial obelisk, dedicated 12.5.1986.

Chelmsford Cathedral, Essex, Stained glass windows in south porch.

RAF Museum, Hendon, Memorial honouring all Americans who served in the 8th Air Force in World War II. This was originally dedicated at Liverpool on 28.5.1984 but is now resited at Hendon in the 'Bomber Command' museum.

Museums

96th Bomb Group Memorial Learning Centre

Eccles Hall School, Quidenham, Norfolk
Tel: 095 387 217

One of the buildings which served as the sick headquarters for Snetterton Heath base, home of 96th Bomb Group. It offers an insight into life on the base through books, photographs, videos and various artefacts.

100th Bomb Group Memorial Museum

Thorpe Abbotts, Norfolk
Tel: 0379 870837

Housed in the 100th Bomb Group original control tower, exhibits include a fine collection of uniforms, photographs, medals, personal documents. Visit also the Chapel of Remembrance and other buildings containing exhibits.

390th Bomb Group Memorial Air Museum

Parham Airfield, Framlingham, Suffolk
Tel: 0379 898085

The control tower was restored by enthusiasts and is now an Aladdin's cave of aviation memorabilia dedicated to the RAF and 8th Air Force. Adjacent is a Nissen hut assembled from original components.

Aerospace Museum

Cosford, Shifnal, Shropshire
Tel: 0902 374112/374872

One of the largest aviation collections in Europe with over 70 aircraft on display including a B-24 Liberator, together with missiles, engines, uniforms and aviation memorabilia.

Airscene Aviation Museum

Blake Hall, Harlow, Essex
Tel: 0245 351116

A collection of aeronautica of the 40s, with a section dedicated to the 9th Air Force and the 387th Bomb Group.

East Essex Aviation Museum

St Osyth, Essex
Tel: 0255 423604/476127

A collection of aircraft brought down over Essex including a P-51 Mustang and parts of a B-17.

Fenland Aviation Museum

West Walton, Wisbech, Cambridgeshire
Tel: 0945 63870

World War II aero engines, memorabilia, uniforms and photographs.

Hardwick Airfield, Norfolk

Tel: 050 844 263

A recently formed museum of World War II aviation archaeology and memorabilia, housed in old Nissen hut on airfield site which was home to the 93rd Bomb Group.

Imperial War Museum

Duxford, Cambridgeshire
Tel: 0223 835000

Europe's top aviation museum with over 120 historic aircraft on display. Many are in flying condition and regularly take to the sky over Duxford. They include examples of the main US combat aircraft of World War II. As well as the existing 8th Air Force display, the construction of the American Air Museum in Britain commences in 1992. This will include many American aeroplanes, educational displays, military equipment, archival research material and special exhibitions on Anglo-American co-operation.

Lincolnshire Aviation Heritage Centre

East Kirkby Airfield, Lincolnshire
Tel: 07903 207

Set to a 1943 theme, the exhibits are well documented and include the remains of a B-24, a P-38 and two B-17s.

Long Shop Museum

Leiston, Suffolk
Tel: 0728 832189

Home base for the 357th Fighter Group, the display deals graphically with the occupation of the airfield by the 357th and its 3 squadrons.

The Muckleburgh Collection

Weybourne Military Camp, Norfolk
Tel: 026 370 210

The largest private collection of militaria with over 3,000 exhibits. Working examples of WWII British/USA tanks, armoured cars, guns, vehicles, searchlights, uniforms etc, are complemented with an extensive model display. Static aircraft and full size lifeboats add another dimension. Veterans admitted free. (See events listing for special Veterans Day on 25th May, '92)

Norfolk and Suffolk Aviation Museum

Flixton, Bungay, Suffolk
Tel: 0508 43778

Includes several complete aircraft, some ex USAAF, as well as a restored Liberator gun turret. Also memorabilia and personal collections.

Norwich Aviation Museum

Norwich Airfield, Norfolk
Tel: 0603 625309

Includes 8 preserved aircraft including a Vulcan bomber and Herald airliner. Comprehensive collection of RAF and USAAF related items.

RAF Museum

Hendon, London
Tel: 081-205-2266

Britain's national museum of aviation displays over 70 famous aircraft, each with their own flying story. Also many scenes from British aviation history including the 'Battle of Britain Experience' and in 1992 the Bomber Command Hall 'USAAF Exhibition' with a B-17G, B-25J, P-51 and American Crew Room and War Memorial.

RAF Wattisham Museum

Wattisham, Suffolk
Tel: 0449 720631 ext 297

Housed in the Nissen hut which was the base church during the war, this collection includes photographs, maps and memorabilia telling the history of RAF Wattisham, including many items of the period when the 479th Fighter Group were there.

Rebel Air Museum

Earls Colne Airfield, Essex
Tel: 081 690 0917 (evenings)

An impressive display including the largest piece of a B-26 in the UK, as well as other aeroplane parts, many items of memorabilia, uniforms and photographs. Mostly devoted to the 9th Air Force.

Seething Control Tower

Seething, Norfolk
Tel: 0508 50787

Former home of the 448th Bomb Group, the renovated control tower exhibits (on the first Sunday in the month from April to September) mission diaries, personal stories, photographs and wartime mementoes. (See events listing for special 2nd Air Division Open Day on 6th September 1992).

The Shuttleworth Collection

Old Warden Aerodrome, Nr Biggleswade, Bedfordshire
Tel: 076 727 288

The Shuttleworth Collection is a quintessentially English illustration of the lifetime achievements of Richard Shuttleworth, a motor racing driver and aviator extraordinary.

The Squadron

North Weald Airfield, Epping, Essex
Tel: 037 882 4510/12

Built to represent a WWII RAF station, this is home to vintage and historic aircraft including the Harvard Formation team and the Great War combat team. Fully operational RAF mess/bar.

Tangmere Military Aviation Museum Trust

Tangmere Airfield, Chichester, West Sussex
Tel: 0243 775223

The museum tells the story of Military Flying from the earliest days to the present time and includes photographs etc, relating to the 31st Fighter Group of the US 8th Air Force.

Tower Museum

RAF Bassingbourn, Cambridgeshire
Tel: 0462 673340

Run by the East Anglian Aviation Society as a memorial to those who flew from the base, 99% of the artefacts on show are genuine material. The first floor is devoted to the 91st Bomb Group.

Holbrook, Suffolk.

East Anglia

East Anglia is a great curve of land jutting bluntly into the North Sea. Once thickly forested and bounded by marshland, it has always been a place a little apart from the mainstream. The land is fertile, the sea fruitful, the people humorous and down to earth. Today's East Anglia is tagged 'the fastest growing region of Britain', but our rich history still shapes and influences the people and the place. Neolithic man walked the sandy heaths of Breckland, where at Grimes Graves you can creep into flint mine shafts 4,000 years old. At Cockley Cley, there's a reconstructed Iceni Village. This pre-Roman tribe selected a site with a spring of water so pure that it has been used to help people with the '20th century disease' - total allergy syndrome. Colchester was the Roman capital of Britain, trading in corn and cattle, slaves and pearls, and Lavenham is the best example of a small medieval town that you will find anywhere.

Buy why go on about history? It's the East Anglia of the 1990s that you'll be visiting. Those of you who knew us in the 40s may find that not so much has changed. More cars, certainly, new houses, bigger fields and fewer hedges, but the underlying fabric is still the same. Soft summer colours, bluebell woods, little river valleys, great churches full of light and soaring wooden angels, pastel washed houses and thatched cottages round a village green. We still have Harvest Suppers and village fetes, barn dances and carol concerts. Village social life still revolves around the church and the pub (not always in that order!). Welcome back!

Above: Castle Hedingham.

Right: Colchester Castle.

Essex

Bordering London to the south, Essex is a county of surprising contrasts. The busy towns of Chelmsford and Basildon lie cheek by jowl with whimsically named villages like Abbess Roding, Good Easter and Loves Green. Neat white painted weatherboard cottages sit comfortably with soft red brick and colour-washed houses, and the leafy hornbeam glades and pools of Epping Forest still spread their shade right into the suburbs of London.

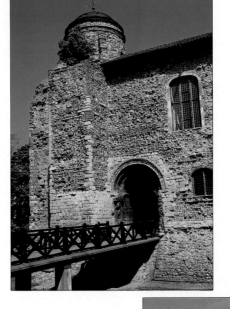

Towns like Billericay and Witham are so close to London, and yet their main streets still have the atmosphere of a small country town on market day. Streets are lined with old brick and plaster buildings, some pretty, some elegant, most pleasing to the eye. Saffron Walden is lovely. The Middle Ages brought wealth through wool and trading in the saffron from which the town takes its name. The High Street and Bridge Street are lined with many fine buildings decorated with carved beams and ornate plasterwork, home to a wide variety of shops selling things like second hand books and old prints. On the common, you can thread your way back in time through the sinuous concentric circles of a rare turf maze. Nearby Thaxted made its money from cutlery rather than wool, and in the 14th and 15th centuries was one of the richest towns in Essex. Built on a hill, the glorious steeple of St John the Baptist

Southend-on-Sea.

Church soars over the little town. Thaxted's 15th century Guildhall stands at the bottom of the hill, white plaster and silvered beams, beautiful in its simplicity. Climb up the narrow ladders in John Webb's windmill: from the top of the red brick tower you can see the town nestled in a landscape as soft and curving as a goosedown quilt.

There are some lovely village greens in Essex. Finchingfield is the most famous. Ducks bob on a white-railed pond and the village street winds gently up the hill to the church. Perfection! In contrast, Writtle is hardly ever visited by tourists but it, too, has a tree-fringed pond on a village green surrounded by ancient houses and with the church in the background. The church, by the way, has a great number of brasses, mostly dating from the 1500s.

Like Suffolk and Norfolk, Essex has a long coastline. The tide gurgles over miles of saltmarsh, creeks and river estuaries. Smuggling was once a way of life here, and the Peter Boat Inn at Leigh-on-Sea was one of their many hiding places for contraband. Other Essex pubs include the picturesque Peldon Rose, the beamed White Harte and Woolpack Inn, both at Coggeshall, and the Swan at Great Henny with its lawns running down to the river. Fresh fish is a great feature of menus throughout the county,

Suffolk

Hay is still cut on Mellis common; sweet, green, fragrant and full of wildflowers. Mellis itself is typical of this deeply rural county - just a collection of ancient farmhouses and cottages around a sweetly stretching village green. Ipswich is the county town. A Saxon port on the River Orwell, it retains something of its character around the dock, still home to black hulled barges like the Phonoecian and where medieval merchants' and captains' houses still surround the busy quay. Just out of the town centre is Christchurch Mansion, lying in its parkland like a beautiful red brick Elizabethan dolls' house with rooms furnished in different periods. What's more, entry is free of charge - an absolute bargain!

Left: The East Anglian Railway Museum.

and you can watch the fishermen at work off the beach in places like Old Leigh near Southend -on-Sea. The little port of Maldon is home to many of the old sailing barges. Their great black hulls and towering masts line the Hythe as they did in so many East Anglian ports 50 years ago. The seaside holiday is still a great British tradition - although many Britons now prefer the warmth of the Mediterranean to the chilly North Sea - and resorts like Southend and Clacton (both on-Sea) are still the choice for many a family holiday.

Constable Country, on the Essex/Suffolk border is the area once beloved by John Constable, one of our most famous landscape painters. Willow-shaded watermeadows, the deep green river, Flatford Mill and Willy Lott's cottage are little changed since Constable's time. A favourite way to spend a sunny afternoon is to walk along the river from Flatford and revel in a sumptuous cream tea at the Essex Rose tearoom in Dedham. During Harvest Festival, Dedham's great gleaming wool church is filled with the produce of this rich agricultural area: apples and grain, vegetables and flowers. Dedham is beautiful, the red brick and timbered buildings forming a whole that is totally pleasing to the eye, the river flowing between leafy banks, and cricketers on the village green on a summer Sunday afternoon. What more perfect place to end your tour of Essex or, indeed, to begin it?

You'll find some lovely pubs in Suffolk. The Peacock at Chelsworth is probably everyone's dream of a country inn, pink-washed with a flower-filled garden and serving good food. The Scole Inn, a handsome coaching inn on the Ipswich - Norwich road, is stunning inside with big log fires, carved beams and very good food. The story goes that a local highwayman escaped capture by riding his horse up the stairs and into one of the bedrooms - and they can show you the hoof prints to prove it! This inn, not surprisingly, has a haunted bedroom, although the ghost is human and not equine. Likewise, the Saracen's Head at Newton Green. The old pub games of skittles and shove ha'penny have mostly disappeared but you can get a game of darts in any village pub. The Jolly Sailor at Orford has a shove ha'penny board, and you can pit your skill against the locals. Southwold is the home of East Anglian beer. The Victoria at Earl Soham brews its own beer, and the Queen's Head at Brandeston is a good example of an unpretentious and un-spoilt village pub - and they do good pub grub, too.

The estuary of the River Orwell is reputed to be one of the most beautiful in England. Crossed now by the soaring spans of the Orwell Bridge, the river is channelled by low tree-topped cliffs, fields and bird-rich marshes. The view from the cliffs at Nacton is good for the soul: the little

Above: Snape Maltings Concert Hall.

Left: Boxford.

sandy beach, quiet water
and boats bobbing at their
mid-river moorings. On
the opposite bank at
Woolverston, stands the
cottage known at Cat
House. Legend has it that a
painted silhouette of a
white cat was placed in the
window to give smugglers
the all clear.

Suffolk's Heritage
Coast has so many places
you shouldn't miss. Orford
is one of them. The massive
keep of the castle, started in
1165 for Henry II, broods
over this elegant little town. Within these great
grey stone walls was imprisoned the Orford
Merman - half man and half fish - a legend
already old in the 15th century. The poor merman was 'put to torments' but refused to talk
like a Christian and eventually managed to
escape out to sea, never to be seen again (and
who could blame him?). The Pinney family,
who have adopted the merman as their symbol,
run the Butley Orford Oysterage on the market
place. A place of pilgrimage for lovers of sea-
food, it is renowned for its smoked salmon and
local oysters. The Pinneys' smokehouses stand
on the banks of Butley Creek, and this is where
their boats still land their catch.

Norfolk

A visit to Norfolk really has to include Norwich. Built of luminous Caen stone, ferried in barges all the way from France, the cathedral was begun in 1096. Pull's Ferry, a perfectly proportioned grey flint arch, guards what was once the watergate from the river to the cathedral site. The 15th century spire soars over 300 feet above the Cathedral Close which is a mass of fragrant cherry blossom in the spring. It used to be said that in Norwich you could visit a different church every Sunday of the year, and a different pub every night of the year - and it's not far short of that today! Many of the churches are now reduntant, but they still play a part in the modern community. St Peter Hungate houses a brass rubbing museum and displays of church art and furnishings; Little St James has been imaginatively converted into Norwich's delightful Puppet Theatre; St Gregory's has a fine example of a sanctuary knocker, which gave the fugitive protection if he could touch it before being caught. Elm Hill, cobbled and lined with fine timbered houses, slopes and twists down to Tombland and gives

the modern visitor an idea of what the medieval city might have been like. Among the many specialist shops is Colman's Mustard Shop in Bridewell Alley. Colman's have milled mustard for over 160 years and this lovely little shop contains a museum of mustard making. You can get every variety of mustard known to man - from some to put on your roast beef, to some to put in your footbath! Take a ride on one of the Southern River Steamers boats. Cedric Lovell will take you through the heart of the city where the River Wensum reveals secret courtyards, green lanes and gardens never seen from the road.

The Norfolk Broads lie to the North East of the city. For centuries, Norwich was England's second city and the population's insatiable need for fuel caused the formation of this unique landscape. Formed by the natural flooding of the medieval peat-diggings, the lakes and rivers of the Broads are, of course, best explored by boat, although the road runs over a causeway at Filby and Ormesby Broads and provides marvellous views for motorists. For the boating visitor, the popular holiday areas are well signposted - by poles stuck in the water at river junctions! Visit the Broads Authority's Toad Hole Cottage Museum at Ludham. This tiny cottage will give you an idea of the marshman's life around 100 years ago. Norfolk reed is considered to be the best thatching material, and acres of whispering sedge are still harvested by boat in the traditional way. The windmills to be seen on the Broads are, almost without exception, drainage pumps rather than corn mills and Berney Arms Mill is a working example. 70ft high, its round black tower and white sails dominate the lonely skyline at Halvergate Marshes.

Above: The Stracey Arms Mill, Norfolk.

Left: Blakeney Quay

The beach at Great Yarmouth.

Cambridgeshire

pay special attention to Emmanuel College. An ex-student, John Harvard, sailed for America in 1636 where, on his death, he bequeathed half his estate (£779 17s 2d) and 320 books to found Harvard College. The Backs, the college gardens, are a mass of daffodils and crocuses in Spring and the river is perfect at any time of year. Scudamore's Boatyard hires punts, but beware - punting is more difficult than it looks.

Cambridgeshire is rich in beautiful cities. On the north western edge of East Anglia's flat Fenland is Peterborough. Another cathedral, this time set in a wide and handsome city square, ancient buildings and narrow streets. The shopping is excellent. The Queensgate shopping centre has some of the best stores and was voted the most attractive small shopping centre in Europe. Flag Fen, near Peterborough, allows you to see a genuine Bronze Age island-village with wooden houses 3,000 years old resurrected from their watery resting place at the bottom of a lake.

Although the southern part of Cambridgeshire is attractive, mostly wide rolling fields of wheat or barley, it's the Fens that are special. Once an eerie, hushed place of marsh and secret waterways, the Fens were drained in the 17th century to provide some of the most fertile farmland in Britain. Flat but not featureless (although it has been said that the true Fenman has only one reaction when he sees a tree - he reaches for his axe), this is a strange world where rivers are raised high above the shrunken land and places have outlandish names like Ten Mile Bank, Euximoor Fen and Three Holes.

Cambridgeshire, sometimes neglected by the visitor to East Anglia, has some of the most distinctive countryside to be seen in Britain. In 1912 Rupert Brooke, the First World War poet, wrote of Grantchester near Cambridge "Say, is there Beauty yet to find? And Certainty? and Quiet kind? Deep meadows yet, for to forget The lies, and truths, and pain? ... oh! yet Stands the Church clock at ten to three? And is there honey still for tea?" The answer is still "Yes".

Ely is not so much of a city, perhaps, more a busy market town, but the glorious cathedral gives Ely its city status. Begun in 1083, the cathedral stands clustered round with buildings on one side and edging green, sheep-grazed meadows on the other. They charge visitors to go in, but it's worth it. The Lady Chapel is the best example of Decorated architecture in Britain; the Prior's Door a moving mix of pagan and barbaric Norman carving; the great Lantern Tower a marvel of medieval engineering suspending mighty oak beams over 60ft high above a lofty light-filled nave.

Not 20 miles away, lies Cambridge. A famous university city since the first college, Peterhouse, was founded in 1281, Cambridge is all that you would expect. Extremely busy, bursting at the seams with visitors in the summer: you still have to visit it. The colleges, handsome, elegant, and beautiful by turns, are set in quiet courtyards, many backing on to the river. The Tourist Information Centre guided tours are a must. Perhaps American visitors might

Above: Punting on the River Cam.

Right: Ely Cathedral.

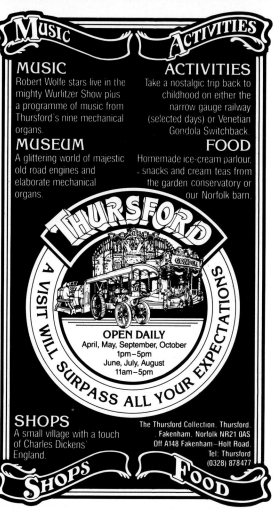

Accommodation

Please see page 113 for an explanation of the Classification and Membership schemes.

Bedfordshire

***M* The Bedford Moat House Hotel,
2 St Marys Street, Bedford MK42 0AR**
Tel: 0234 355131

Ideally located beside the river in the centre of Bedford. 100 rooms all en suite, 2 restaurants, free parking, banqueting for 350, rates £38 pppn including dinner, accommodation and breakfast.

Cambridgeshire

***M* Alconbury House Hotel,
Alconbury Weston, Huntingdon PE17 5JG**
Tel: 0480 890807 👑👑👑

Alconbury House Hotel and restaurant. Bijou hotel of 22 bedrooms with many personal touches. 2 miles from USAF Alconbury main gate.

***M* Arundel House Hotel,
53 Chesterton Road, Cambridge CB4 3AN**
Tel: 0223 67701 👑👑👑 COMMENDED

Elegant 88 bedroom 19th century Victorian terraced hotel, beautifully overlooking the River Cam and open parkland. Only a short walk to the city centre and famous university and colleges. The restaurant has a reputation for some of the best food in the area and yet prices are very reasonable. Single room £35.00 - £51.50, double room £52.00 - £69.50, all with private facilities.

***M* The Gonville Hotel,
Gonville Place, Cambridge CB1 1LY**
Tel: 0223 66611 👑👑👑👑 COMMENDED

Americans 1992 - 'The Gonville' occupies one of the favourable positions, walking distance Colleges and city centre. Excellent cuisine, rooms en suite and all the amenities. Single £63.50, double or twin £79.00 inclusive of English breakfast and VAT.

Essex

2 The Chase, Straight Road, Lexden, Colchester
Tel: 0206 540587 Listed COMMENDED

See a piece of real England. Superb 60 year old house of character with beautiful secluded gardens. Three spacious twin bedrooms (2 ground floor); en suite facilities; large comfortable lounges with TV. Bed & breakfast £20 single, £35 double.

11 Harvest End, Stanway, Colchester CO3 5YX
Tel: 0206 43202 Listed

Family house, quiet position, situated just outside the historical town of Colchester, easy access for A12 to London. Coffee/tea making facilities and TV in all rooms. £16.00-£18.00 single, £30.00-£32.00 double.

***M* Miami Motel,
Princes Road, Chelmsford CM2 9AJ**
Tel: 0245 269603 👑👑👑👑 APPROVED

A family run motel with 57 bedrooms all en suite, direct dial telephone, TV, radio, trouser press, teasmade and Sky TV. Restaurant and bar open to non residents. All rooms double/twin size let as singles. Ample free parking. Only 3 mins from London by train. Chelmsford is also very central for all of Essex by road and rail.

***M* Old House Bed & Breakfast,
Fordstreet, Aldham, Colchester CO6 3PH**
Tel: 0206 240456 Listed COMMENDED

Stay in a genuine 14th century historic house, now a comfortable family home with oak beams, log fires and no unfriendly ghosts. Large garden, ample parking and aircraft-enthusiast host! Easy access Wormingford, Earls Colne, Gosfield, Boxted, Birch etc. 5m west of Colchester on A604.

***M* Quietwaters Hotel Golf & Country Club,
Colchester Road, Tolleshunt Knights, Maldon CM9 8HX**
Tel: 0621 868888

A luxury hotel set in 320 acres of beautiful countryside. Facilities include a Links and a Championship course, Leadbetter golf academy, tennis, squash, bowls and a health club and pool.

Hertfordshire

M Briggens House Hotel, Briggens Park, Stanstead Road (A414), Stanstead Abbotts, Ware SG12 8LD

Tel: 0279 792416

Set in 80 acres of beautifully landscaped parkland boasting a 9 hole professional golf course, tennis courts and swimming pool. With 54 individually designed bedrooms. The Bridgeman restaurant features imaginative yet classical cuisine following the time honoured traditions of impeccable hospitality. Whether staying for business or pleasure Briggens House offers the best welcome for miles around.

M Down Hall Hotel, Hatfield Heath, Bishops Stortford CM22 7AS

Tel: 0279 731441

Victorian country house hotel set in extensive grounds, 103 luxurious bedrooms, indoor and outdoor leisure facilities. 8 miles from Stansted airport. Double rooms from £123.00.

Norfolk

M Knights Hill Hotel, South Wootton, Kings Lynn

Tel: 0553 675566 COMMENDED

Sympathetically converted farm complex with hotel, traditional pub, two restaurants, health and leisure club, conference facilities. Close to historic Kings Lynn, Sandringham, West Norfolk countryside and coast.

23 Market Place, Hingham, Norwich NR9 4AF

Tel: 0953 850398 Listed COMMENDED

Our 400 year old ground floor accommodation offers comfort, privacy and old-world ambience. £50 a night (double) includes traditional breakfast served in your beamed room with inglenook fireplace. Picturesque Hingham (14m West of Norwich) is centrally placed for easy access to all bases (Deopham 2m) and has historic ties with USA (Abraham Lincoln). Local tours using 1932 Talbot Saloon offered. Further upstairs double room available.

Aylsham Motel, Norwich Road, Aylsham, Norwich NR11 6JH

Tel: 0263 734851 APPROVED

Family run, purpose built motel with all rooms en suite and bar and restaurant facilities available. Situated 10m North of Norwich within easy reach of many war-time airfields. Single £33.50, double £46.50 including full breakfast.

M Maranatha Guest House, 115 Gaywood Road, King's Lynn PE30 2PU

Tel: 0553 774596

Large carrstone and brick licensed residence. Friendly, personal service. Gardens front and rear. TVs, complimentary tea and coffee all rooms. AA, RAC, 2 Crown. Close to coast and Sandringham. Accessible for Marham-Sculthorpe-Mildenhall-Lakenheath. Double from £20, single from £15.

M Marlborough House Hotel, 22 Stracey Road (off Thorpe Road), Norwich NR1 1EZ

Tel: 0603 628005

A long established well appointed family run hotel. Close to city centre. (Railway station 2 mins). All bedrooms have tea/coffee making facilities, colour TV. Double/family rooms have ensuite facilities. Tariff includes full English breakfast. Prices on request. Car park.

Norfolk Country Cousins, Point House, Mill Common Road, Ridlington, North Walsham NR28 9TY

Tel: 0692 650286

All over Norfolk self-catering cottage holidays to suit every mood, 2-8 people coastal or country, comfortable and well equipped, plus bike hire and picnic hampers. Or cycling breaks with panache! 2 nights in each port of call, luggage transported by us. Brochures on request.

M Searles Holiday Centre, South Beach Road, Hunstanton PE36 5BB

Tel: 0485 534211

This family run holiday centre is situated on Norfolk's West coast, 250 yards from the beach. Our accommodation includes 35' x 12' holiday homes of the latest design and comfort whether you wish to relax in our swimming area, indoor/outdoor, or enjoy our entertainment complex you will be made very welcome. Cost per week: £200-£350 for 6 people.

Norwich and Norfolk Holiday Homes, 18 Keswick Road, Cringleford, Norwich NR4 6UG

Tel: 0603 503389   Fax: 0603 55123

Wide range self-catering accommodation (including bungalows equipped for the disabled) in city and county. We offer a friendly, comprehensive service. Please write or phone for free brochure.

Sherbourne House Hotel, Norwich Road, Attleborough NR17 2JX

Tel: 0953 454363

Sherbourne House is a delightful Georgian family run hotel situated in central Norfolk. The hotel is famed for its cuisine and fine Australian wine list. The majority of the rooms are en suite and some have four posters. Double rooms from £42 per night. AA 2 Star.

Wash & Tope Hotel, Le-strange Terrace, Hunstanton

Tel: 0485 532250

Small family run hotel overlooking the sea. Fully licensed bar and restaurant open all year. Central heating, en suite rooms. Ideal base for touring. Sandringham 6 miles. Prices from £15 per person bed and breakfast. AA 1 Star.

Northamptonshire

M Holiday Inn Garden Court, Northampton/Bedford Road, Northampton NN4 0YF

Tel: 0604 22777

We offer 104 superb bedrooms featuring double beds, en suite bathrooms, individually controlled air-conditioning, colour TV and in-room movies. Direct dial telephones, plus tea and coffee making facilities. £37.50 per room during August.

Suffolk

The Bell Hotel, High Street, Saxmundham, Suffolk IP17 1AB

Tel: 0728 602331

18th century coaching inn, situated in a quiet Suffolk market town. 14 rooms, many with private facilities. Quiet, comfortable, relaxed, excellent food (with an Italian flavour), extensive wine list and real beers. Well remembered by the Yoxford Boys of wartime fame.

M Cakes & Ale, Abbey Lane, Leiston IP16 4TE

Tel: 0728 831655

357th Fighter Group Leiston. Base now holiday homes and campground called 'Cakes & Ale', with clubhouse named 'Yoxford Boys' tribute to 357th. Visitors welcome to call in or stay on campground. From £10 per night.

Cobbs Hall, Great Saxham, Bury St Edmunds IP29 5JN

Tel: 0284 850678

Listed

Traditional English country house, two day breaks full board and guided tours of the area and historic Bury St Edmunds. Very comfortable accommodation with superb English cooking from £130 per person.

M Crown and Castle Hotel, Orford IP12 2LJ

Tel: 0395 450205

COMMENDED

Single room bed and breakfast £32.50, double room bed and breakfast £55.00. An old timbered coaching inn, opposite the castle. All bedrooms have television, telephone, tea/coffee making facilities, restaurant open to non-residents. Groups welcomed by arrangement, very friendly atmosphere.

M The Four Horseshoes Country Inn and Hotel, Thornham Magna, Nr Eye

Tel: 0379 71777

COMMENDED

Set betwixt Mendlesham and Eye airfields. The olde worlde bar within with blazing log fires in winter serves a delicious range of home cooked meals and real ales. Dine in our a la carte restaurant or our bar. For lovers of the countryside the horseshoes trail begins and ends at The Shoes.

M Hamling House Hotel, Bull Road, Pakenham, Bury St Edmunds IP31 2LW

Tel: 0359 30934

COMMENDED

Possibly the most re-visited small hotel in the area. Tranquil alpine style country house in picturesque village near historic Bury St Edmunds. All rooms enjoy a superb range of facilities. £38 per person per night half board.

M Hintlesham Hall, Hintlesham, Ipswich IP8 3NS

Tel: 047 387 334

HIGHLY COMMENDED

16th century manor house hotel set in 170 acres of parkland and golf course. Bedrooms from £97 for a double room. Short breaks available.

M Seckford Hall Hotel & Restaurant, Nr Woodbridge
Tel: 0394 385678

👑👑👑 HIGHLY COMMENDED

Close to many wartime airfields, Seckford Hall is a Highly Commended country hotel offering excellent accommodation, cuisine and facilities. A 16th century manor, it is a most beautiful house and the adjacent farm has been skillfully converted to a 'courtyard' of studios and suites. Indoor heated pool complex and 9 hole golf.

M The Smoke House, Beck Row, Mildenhall
Tel: 0638 713223
Fax: 0638 712202

 👑👑👑👑 COMMENDED

Old country inn with friendly atmosphere offering British hospitality at its best. 103 bedrooms (all with private bathroom). Singles available. All rooms have colour TV with video, radio, direct-dial telephone, tea/coffee making facilities, hair dryer, trouser press. Baby listening service. Restaurant, bar, lounge, log fires, TV room, video library with 2,000 titles, 2 dance floors. Fishing, golf, swimming, riding nearby. £82.50 with private bathroom 1 Sept 1991 - 31 March 1992. Price not applicable at Christmas and New Year. Price inc. accommodation for any two nights. Parking available. English/continental breakfast, a daily allowance of £10 per person towards dinner (a la carte).

Suffolk Grange Hotel, Ransomes Europark, Ipswich IP3 9SJ   Tel: 0473 272244

Set in the heart of East Anglia, Suffolk Grange Hotel offers a unique blend of comfort and character. 60 luxuriously equipped bedrooms have en suite bathrooms. Restaurant, sauna, solarium, gym. From £30 per person/night incl breakfast.

M Waverley Hotel, 2 Wolsey Gardens, Felixstowe IP11 7DF
Tel: 0394 282811   👑👑👑

Elegant Victorian hotel overlooking sea and promenade. The hotel has been recently fully refurbished to a very high standard and many rooms have balconies and spectacular sea views. Felixstowe is the ideal base for exploring beautiful, unspoilt Suffolk. Ideal also for ferries.

M Wentworth Hotel, Aldeburgh
Tel: 0728 452312   👑👑👑 COMMENDED

The Wentworth Hotel lies on the edge of the Suffolk Coast at the old fishing town of Aldeburgh and has the comfort and style of a country house with log fires and antique furniture. Aldeburgh is ideal as a touring centre for East Anglia. We have quality shops, 2 excellent golf courses, an abundance of long walks, bird watching at Minsmere and music and arts at the famous Snape Maltings concert hall and, of course, miles of beach to sit upon and watch the sea.

Places to Visit

M Black Sheep Ltd

9 Penfold Street, Aylsham, Norwich, NR11 6ET
Norfolk   Tel: 0263 733124/732006

Where is the Black Sheep Squadron? We don't know, nor does the Pentagon! But come and see us for the very best in British Country Knitwear in pure natural undyed wool. Free colour mail order catalogue on request.

M Lowestoft, Suffolk

Visit Lowestoft and re-live your memories. Things may have changed, but the welcome you'll receive is still the same. For a free colour brochure including accommodation phone: 011 44 502 565989 or write to Tourist Information, Room 2, The Esplanade, Lowestoft, Suffolk NR33 0QF, England.

M Ely Cathedral

Ely, Cambridgeshire

This magnificent 11th Century Cathedral with its surrounding medieval buildings, rises majestically above the city. Stained Glass Museum, with a unique collection of stained glass through the ages (open Easter to October inclusive); guided tours; shops; Refectory; medieval Almonry restaurant. Admission £2.50; concessionary rates for senior citizens, students and pre-booked parties. Contact Jan Pye, The Chapter House, The College, Ely, Cambs CB7 4DN. Tel: 0353 667735

M Brooklands Museum

Weybridge, Surrey

See the Vickers Wellington bomber recovered from Loch Ness, Barnes Wallis' dam-busting 'Bouncing Bomb' and a unique collection of historic aircraft at the birthplace of British aviation. VAFA AERO-PHIL commemorative first day covers are available from the museum shop or by mail order. 30 mins from central London, open weekends. Pre-booked tours Tuesday to Friday. Tel: 0932 857381.

M National Horse Racing Museum

**99 High Street, Newmarket CB8 8WL Suffolk
Tel: 0638 667333**

Housed in Regency subscription rooms, the Museum displays the history and development of horse racing since 1605. Tours of training yards, horse farms and historic sights available. Booking essential. Mar-Dec, Tues - Sun. Also Mons July/August.

National Stud

Newmarket CB8 0XE Suffolk   Tel: 0638 663464

A conducted tour of one of the most prestigious horse farms in the international capital of the racing and breeding industry. See stallions, mares and foals. Open March to October.

The Military Gallery

S E Pasby, 7 Laurel Drive, Long Melford CO10 7JU, Suffolk   Tel: 0787 79927

We feature the aviation and marine art of much acclaimed artist Robert Taylor with limited edition individually signed prints, countersigned by World War II flying aces, naval heroes or similar VIP's. Look for us at many of this year's events. Also sales points at The Muckleburgh Collection, Weybourne.

M Sizewell Visitors Centre

Sizewell Power Station, Leiston, Suffolk Tel: 0728 642139

All ages are fascinated by this insight into the nuclear power industry. Guides will answer your questions. Audio/visual displays to operate yourself. Tours of Sizewell B site arranged. Open daily 10am-4pm (Closed Sundays Oct-March) Free.

M Sacrewell Farm and Country Centre

Sacrewell, Thornhaugh, Peterborough PE8 6HJ, Cambridgeshire   Tel: 0708 782222

8 miles west of Peterborough on the A47. Sacrewell is "always open and always beautiful". This 500 acre farm is 'England for real', with working watermill, gardens, farm animals, bygones and history - all packed with interest. Refreshments and souvenir/gift shop 11am-5.30pm. Admission all visitors over 5 years £1.00. Party visits with simple catering, please enquire David Powell.

M Rollerbury

Station Hill, Bury St Edmunds, Suffolk Tel: 0284 701216

The National Roller Skating Centre. American influenced facilities include DJs, cafe, licensed bar, video games. Easy access by road and rail. Free car and coach park. Strict supervision and great atmosphere make it ideal for families. Prices from £2.00 to £4.30 and group offers are available.

The Squadron

North Weald Airfield, Epping CM16 6AA Essex

The Squadron is a flying museum and has been built to represent a World War II fighter aircraft base. All equipment, buildings, furniture and memorabilia are of that period. In addition there is an authentic NAAFI (restaurant) and squadron mess (bar) available to visitors. Aircraft based at the Squadron include the Harvard formation team, the World War I combat team, P51 Mustangs, Grumman Avenger and B25. For further information and booking telephone 0378 824510.

BATTLEFIELD TOURS, WWI, WW2 and Waterloo destinations.

Fully escorted. Prices from £198. Further details please contact Richard Mason, Blake Mason Historical Tours, 30 Smithfield Road, Norwich NR1 2HN. Tel: 0603 618803

Chauffeuring by Charles

14 Venice Court, Wake Green Park, Moseley, Birmingham B13 9YL
Tel: 021 442 4677   Mobile: 0831 844496

Return to England in style, Rolls Royce 'Silver Shadow'. Exclusive corporate or social service includes; fully trained chauffeur, itinerary planning, negotiable contract for Reunion.

Eastern National Bus Services

Eastern National Ltd, New Writtle Street, Chelmsford CM2 0SD Essex
Tel: 0245 256151

Remember the buses when you were last in Essex? Eastern National's green buses still provide local services around and between the major towns. See Essex and meet its people again with an Essex Ranger day out ticket for £4.50. Purchase them in advance from offices and agents and self-validate them for the date you travel.

Crown Classification

Over 16,000 hotels, guest houses, motels, inns, B&Bs and farmhouses throughout Great Britain now offer the reassurance of a national Crown classification. Every classified establishment is inspected by the Tourist Boards each year to make sure that standards have been maintained.

A lower classification does not imply lower standards.

Listed Clean and comfortable accommodation, although the range of facilities and services may be limited.

Accommodation with additional facilities including washbasins in all bedrooms, a lounge area and use of a telephone.

A wider range of facilities and services, including morning tea/coffee and calls, bedside lights, colour TV in lounge or bedrooms, assistance with luggage.

At least one-third of the bedrooms with ensuite WC and bath or shower, plus easy chair and full length mirror, shoe cleaning facilities and hairdryers available. Hot evening meals available.

At least three-quarters of the bedrooms with ensuite WC and bath or shower plus colour TV, radio and telephone, 24 hour access and lounge service until midnight. Last orders for evening meals 20.30 hours or later.

All bedrooms having WC, bath and shower ensuite, valet service plus a wide range of facilities and services, including room service, all night lounge service and laundry service. Restaurant open for breakfast, lunch and dinner.

Quality Commendations

To help you find accommodation that offers even higher standards than those required for a simple classification, the tourist boards have introduced three levels of quality commendation, using the terms APPROVED, COMMENDED and HIGHLY COMMENDED. Those establishments that apply for a quality commendation are subject to a more rigorous inspection, which takes into account such important aspects as warmth of welcome, atmosphere and efficiency of service, as well as the quality of furnishings, fitments and equipment.

Key Ratings

Over 10,000 self-catering holiday homes are inspected by the tourist boards and are Key Classified. The range of facilities and equipment provided is indicated by one to five keys. Holiday homes can also apply to be quality commended (see above).

British Graded Holiday Parks Scheme

Over 1,000 holiday parks (caravans, chalets and camping parks) offer the reassurance of a national Q-for quality grade. There are five grades indicated by 1-5 Ticks. The more Ticks the higher the quality standard. Even a small, quiet park with few facilities can achieve five Ticks if what it offers is to an exceptionally high quality standard.

M denotes membership of the Tourist Board.

Tourist Information Centres

Tourist Information Centres offer information on things to do and see, places to eat, and facilities for the elderly and disabled. They will book accommodation for you, either in their own area or further afield, using the 'Book A Bed Ahead Scheme'.

* Not open all year.

Aldeburgh, Suffolk
*The Cinema, High Street Tel: (0728) 453637

Beccles, Suffolk
*The Quay, Fen Lane Tel: (0502) 713196

Bedford, Bedfordshire
10 St Pauls Square Tel: (0234) 215226

Bishop's Stortford, Hertfordshire
2 The Causeway Tel: (0279) 655261 Ext 251

Braintree, Essex
Town Hall Centre, Market Square
Tel: (0376) 550066

Bury St Edmunds, Suffolk
The Athenaeum, Angel Hill Tel: (0284) 764667

Cambridge, Cambridgeshire
Wheeler Street Tel: (0223) 322640

Chelmsford, Essex
County Hall, Market Road Tel: (0245) 283400

Clacton-on-Sea, Essex
23 Pier Avenue Tel: (0255) 423400

Colchester, Essex
1 Queen Street Tel: (0206) 712920

Cromer, Norfolk
*Bus Station, Prince of Wales Road
Tel: (0263) 512497

Diss, Norfolk
Meres Mouth, Mere Street Tel: (0379) 650523

Ely, Cambridgeshire
Oliver Cromwell's House, 29 St Mary's Street
Tel: (0353) 662062

Fakenham, Norfolk
*Red Lion House, Market Place
Tel: (0328) 851981

Felixstowe, Suffolk
Sea Front Tel: (0394) 276770

Great Yarmouth, Norfolk
Town Hall Tel: (0493) 846345
*Marine Parade Tel: (0493) 842195

Hadleigh, Suffolk
Toppesfield Hall Tel: (0473) 822922

Harwich, Essex
Parkeston Quay Tel: (0255) 506139

Hoveton, Norfolk
*Station Road Tel: (0603) 782281

Hunstanton, Norfolk
*The Green Tel: (0485) 532610

Huntingdon, Cambridgeshire
The Library, Princes Street (0480) 425831

Ipswich, Suffolk
Town Hall, Princes Street Tel: (0473) 258070

King's Lynn, Norfolk
The Old Gaol House, Saturday Market Place
Tel: (0553) 763044

Lavenham, Suffolk
*The Guildhall, Market Place
Tel: (0787) 248207

Lowestoft, Suffolk
*The Esplanade Tel: (0502) 523000/565989

Maldon, Essex
*Maldon Maritime Centre, The Hythe
Tel: (0621) 856503

Mundesley, Norfolk
*2a Station Road Tel: (0263) 721070

Northampton, Northamptonshire
10 St Giles Square Tel: (0604) 22677

Norwich, Norfolk
The Guildhall, Gaol Hill Tel: (0603) 666071

Peterborough, Cambridgeshire
45 Bridge Street Tel: (0733) 317336

Ranworth, Norfolk
*The Staithe Tel: (060549) 453

Saffron Walden, Essex
1 Market Place Tel: (0799) 524282

Sheringham, Norfolk
*Station Approach Tel: (0263) 824329

Southend-on-Sea, Essex
Information Bureau, High Street Precinct
Tel: (0702) 355120
Civic Centre, Victoria Avenue
Tel: (0702) 355122

Southwold, Suffolk
*Town Hall Tel: (0502) 724729

Stowmarket, Suffolk
Wilkes Way Tel: (0449) 676800

Sudbury, Suffolk
*Information Caravan in Station Road
Tel: (0787) 881320

Walsingham, Norfolk
*Shirehall Museum, Common Place
Tel: (0328) 820510

Walton-on-the-Naze, Essex
*Princess Esplanade Tel: (0255) 675542

Wells-next-the-Sea, Norfolk
*Wells Centre, Staithe Street Tel: (0328) 710885

Wisbech, Cambridgeshire
District Library, Ely Place Tel: (0945) 583263